success
WITH LESS™

Releasing Obligations & Discovering Joy

KAREN MANGIA

Published by Marie Street Press
11152 Westheimer Road, Suite 143
Houston, TX 77042
Tel: 832-736-8945
mariestreetpress.com

Cover art designed by: Brenda Phelps Shih

ISBN: 978-0-9854148-7-0
Library of Congress Control Number has been applied for.

Advance Praise For Success With Less

There's no greater gift than good health. Karen's journey to find herself is one that anybody can relate to—she shares advice that's more than just diet, exercise and career. It's advice about life—a life with no regrets. No matter where you are and no matter what life throws at you, this book will make a difference.

Sherrie Bossung, RN, MBA
Vice President, Lilly Foundation

Counter-intuitive and powerful. *Success With Less* shows how to keep moving forward with ease and confidence, even in the toughest circumstances.

Gary Ginstling
CEO of the Indianapolis Symphony Orchestra

Travel with Karen as she shares her personal journey of how she released her "should do's" and began investing her time and energy on her true mission: becoming her amazing authentic self.

Diane Rupert
President, The Rupert Group, Inc.

Karen Mangia gets things done. Good things for people she knows well, and people she may never even meet. With the heart of a servant leader, keen insight and a strong intellect, Karen offers a productive, healthy way forward.

Christina Hale
Indiana State Representative and
Candidate for Lieutenant Governor 2016

Why didn't this book exist already? Brilliant! In the world of books melding personal and professional wellness, this book provides a new (and desperately needed) perspective. *Success With Less* is both practical and inspiring.

Michael Pettry,
Executive Director, Indianapolis Symphonic Choir

The definition of *Success* has been driven by the culture of corporate America since the start of the Industrial Revolution. Karen re-frames the need to succeed with a fresh perspective that *everyone* should understand—and use—to start benchmarking their careers and personal lives. Coming from a high-achieving woman who has worked for Fortune 100 companies (with an incredible story both in and out of the corner office), Karen provides us the valuable insights on how *Less* makes life balanced and compete.

Stephen Jones, Ph.D.
Director of the Center for Information and Communication Studies, Ball State University

Working closely with Karen over the last 20 years, I saw only the overachieving success part of her story. The fact that she had been leveraging the methodology she discusses here—to overcome many of the obstacles that she endured so gracefully—is testament to its power and its impact in her life.

Jeff Cristee
Vice President Worldwide Sales Training and Development, Cisco Systems

This book takes the tricky stuff of life—relationships, career management, health, diet and wellness—and offers a powerful formula for simplifying all of it. And thanks to Karen's candid storytelling, it's incredibly fun to read.

Sali Christeson
Co-Founder and CEO, Argent

For all of us in the Type-A tribe, who start every day ready to conquer the world... Skip your midlife crisis and read this book. You still can have it all and be happy too, when you're definition of "all" is the right one.

Aliza Hutchison
Director of Business Transformation, SolomonEdwards

We've all been at a crossroads in life. In *Success With Less,* Karen shows courage and vulnerability in talking about the hard lessons she has learned in her health, work and relationships. Thanks for sharing your story with us, Karen. It is a shining light unto the path of all who will read and enable.

James Blum, Partner, Strategic Sales Advisors,
Former Vice President of Sales Operations, Cisco Systems

Life throws crisis moments at all of us—those crossroads we all have to face. Karen shows how to move forward, even in the toughest circumstances. Her story is powerful, because it's a story for everyone.

Randy Pond, Former EVP Operations, Cisco

To Diane,

Without your encouragement,
there would be no journey,
no discovery,
no formula,
no book.

Table of Contents

FOREWORD

When you think of family, what comes to mind?

You've probably heard of the Hawaiian word for family: *Ohana. Ohana* represents the idea that families—related or chosen—are bound together, and that members feel a sense of responsibility for one another. In order to be an effective member of a family—any family— you have to make sure that you are able to be your best. You have to be your true self.

At Salesforce, the culture of *Ohana* extends beyond our team members—my colleagues—to include our customers, our partners, and our communities. That's our family.

When we collectively live our *Ohana* culture, we bring our core values to life: Trust, Customer Success, Innovation, Giving Back, Equality, Wellness, Transparency, and Fun. That is how we win together. Sharing our culture with our customers—extending our *Ohana*—is part of our mission.

What I've learned in the process of living these values with our employees, our customers, and our partners every day, is that *Ohana* is a gift you must give yourself first. I'm living proof. Bringing the *Ohana* culture to life with my own team is my top strategic priority. That's why I decided to lead by example and enjoy my first Salesforce-supported sabbatical.

How did I press pause on my dream job long enough to give myself the gift of a break? By building a talented team around me and then empowering them to act on my behalf.

Pressing pause, even for a few months, was a powerful tool. I finally had time to focus on my family, my personal goals, and embrace a new vision of myself. Finding time for the important stuff made me a better leader, a better partner, a better parent, and a better friend.

Each year our Dreamforce event showcases the power of what is possible when you reach beyond your limits, your boundaries, and your labels. When you open your mind to your potential, and embrace the possibilities. When you consider how you can heal the world. When you dream big.

That's what I love about *Success With Less*. Karen had the courage to dream big and then boldly share the setbacks she has overcome. As one of our Salesforce employees, she is living our culture by extending our *Ohana* to you, through this book. In her journey to find a more meaningful measure of success, she has taken time to share what matters most to her.

Whether you're trying to improve your calendar, your career, your relationships or your health, this book will help guide you on your journey. You owe it to yourself—and to your family—to consider a new definition of success. Because healing the world might not be as difficult as you think, especially if you just start with yourself.

Dream Big,

Kristen Engelhardt
Vice President, Voice of the Customer
Salesforce

1

Success With Less

If you came over to my house, I would probably cook you dinner.

When I'm hosting a dinner party, I spend hours planning the menu and executing a series of delectable dishes. I'm amazed at how frequently guests tell me their favorite dish of the evening was the one with the fewest ingredients that took the least amount of time to prepare. A grilled peach half-stuffed with blue cheese and drizzled with balsamic vinegar. Or a raw corn salad with fresh tomatoes, herbs, and olive oil.

Perhaps those humble foods take us back to a simpler time. Or, perhaps you truly can produce a better result using fewer ingredients.

My earliest memories involve food (with a name like Mangia, that's expected!).

From a very early age, I wondered about success.

Beyond being a "good girl," I wondered, *What makes someone "successful?"*

In my formative years, I believed the best predictor of success was a high activity level with the occasional addition of "people pleasing."

I tested the hypothesis:

Activity level + People pleasing = Success

During high school, I repeatedly volunteered at school and in the community, and worked two jobs. I got good grades, won awards... even landed college scholarships.

As I carried the Activity level + People pleasing = Success "formula" forward into college and my adult life, I realized I only knew how to succeed by doing and being "more."

More responsibilities. More employees. More community involvement. More gold stars.

More pleasing, more performing, more perfecting.

One day, I hit the wall—with my foot still on the gas pedal.

My career success reached a plateau. My health simultaneously hit rock bottom.

I realized I couldn't do more.

The success formula that delivered results numerous times was no longer sustainable. Or effective. Or enjoyable.

If I couldn't keep doing more, what could I do instead?

The only reasonable option was "less." But how?

I'm guessing you know how that feels, when what has worked for you in the past is no longer delivering the results you desperately desire— when your formula for personal and professional success stops working—it's exhausting.

Frightening.

Overwhelming.

That's probably why you're here now.

I know how you feel. When you can't achieve the life you envision, and there's not enough time in the day to get it all done, it feels like a prison cell. You're trapped. Boxed in. Limited. Disappointed.

Eventually, hopeless.

The good news is those feelings don't have to linger! You don't have to be trapped by time. That feeling of "overload" doesn't have to define you or limit you.

If you're willing to let go of old ideas and what has made you successful in the past, you, too, can take a new look at old problems. You can find and achieve *Success With Less*.

That's exactly what I had to do. One moment at a time. One commitment at a time. One problem at a time. Until what trapped me in the "overload" gave me the keys to my freedom.

And now I'm offering those keys to you.

Are you ready to be set free?

2

Playing Doctor

If you have your health, you have everything.

How many times have you heard that saying?

It seems reasonable, doesn't it? Almost too easy. So much so that we casually clink our glasses together from time to time to toast good health. *Salud*! *A votre santé!*

I believed I would always have my health. And, therefore, have everything. OK, maybe not always, but at least in my early years.

And that good health was achievable even while taking great liberties with how I treated my body. My stress level. My eating habits. My sleep habits.

After all, I was young "enough." Healthy "enough." Fit "enough." Social "enough." I was even a vegetarian. I thought I would always have "enough" energy to cope with the demands of day-to-day life.

Until one day I didn't.

When I looked in the mirror, I saw a reasonably healthy person. Bright, blue eyes. Long, full head of hair. Clear complexion. Sure, I could lose a few pounds...but, couldn't we all?

What I saw on the outside failed to reflect what was happening on the inside. And I *desperately* wanted to believe what I saw in the mirror.

My appearance deceived me.

The truth was, I treated my body like a bottomless savings account.

Take a red eye flight? Miss a night of sleep? No problem!

Just make a withdrawal from the "sleep bank" for a couple of nights. Then, make a deposit back into the account by sleeping more over the weekend.

A big presentation in the morning? That's easy! Skip your workout out to prepare. Then, skip breakfast to cover the missed workout. Just make another withdrawal from the account. And then promise to exercise longer on Saturday.

It will all balance out in the end.

Until it doesn't.

I found myself playing a dangerous game called "Let's Make a Deal" with my health and well-being. I was an eager contestant on a game show where every point translated to pain, instead of payoff. Because I didn't know the score.

The game seemed like fun. Because I was winning! Promotions, awards, accomplishments...What I didn't realize was: I was competing in a game where, ultimately, no one wins.

Not me. Not you.

I kept playing the game. With gusto.

Eventually, I knew I was running on empty, but I didn't stop.

Or even pause.

Or check my "account balance."

Instead, I gave myself a pep talk. "You can do this! Just a few more days of this crazy schedule. Remember, an object in motion stays in motion!"

A few more days became a few more weeks. A few more weeks became a few more months. A few more months became a habit.

I crisscrossed multiple time zones. Made meals out of packaged snack foods. Missed workouts. Replaced water with coffee. Said yes to every "opportunity."

Until I was living on caffeine. Adrenaline. And fear.

Wait, *fear*?

Why fear?

Well, if I allowed myself to take a break, how long would it take to recover? I was afraid of what would happen if I started saying no.

Would I be overlooked for a promotion? Let my family and friends down? No longer be valuable? Or needed? Or accomplished? Or...loved?

I went from feeling unstoppable to feeling like I couldn't stop. That every aspect of my life was somehow beyond my control. My calendar. My to-do list. My endless obligations.

Instead of thinking or feeling, I was just *doing*. Have you ever been there? I thought I could continue on "fast forward" forever.

My mind started writing checks my body couldn't cash. I was shocked. And perplexed. "How did *this* happen?"

It started with losing my keys.

Every. Single. Day.

I literally could not remember where I left them.

I told myself it was no big deal.

Then I would walk into a room and have no idea why I was there. Easy enough to explain away. I was just preoccupied. Tired. Aging. We all forget things now and again, don't we?

Here's what got my attention in a powerful way.

I forgot my brother's name.

And not just forgot. Imagine frantically searching your phone to find your own brother's name. Because even though I could see his face clearly in my mind, I could not connect with his name.

My heart was racing. My palms were sweating. I was in a state of panic.

What is happening to me?

I could not escape the thought that I was losing my mind.

And, maybe I was.

Insanity. It gave me pause.

But, this pause was different.

This pause was...necessary. It might have even been a "full stop" pause. When life happens to us, life forces us to stop. To reconsider. To rethink. You know that full-stop feeling after something so startling happens that you're left with no other choice?

That's where I was in that exact moment. My heart still racing at full force from the panic of forgetting my brother's name, mixed with a concerned curiosity about what might happen next.

And, at the same time, not really wanting to find out what was going on.

My "full stop" pause didn't last long, because I didn't want to think about stopping for more than a few minutes. I was simply "too busy." Places to go. Things to do. People to see. You know the drill.

My old habits were more comfortable. Especially the habit of ignoring anything that presented me with the reality that I might be losing something. For example, my mind.

Memory loss was the first symptom. But there were others. I started gaining weight.

I became a better storyteller to myself. "You've been eating junk food at the airport. Start packing an apple in your carry on." "You're spending too much time sitting at a desk. Move more." "You're eating too many carbs. Eat more vegetables." "It's the dead of winter. Everyone gains a few pounds in the winter."

What stories do you repeatedly tell yourself? I learned that writing fiction, a "make believe" story, can be very dangerous when it comes to your health.

Especially if you believe your own story.

Next came the fatigue. The system that had worked so well in the past—withdrawal, withdrawal, withdrawal, *deposit!*—failed me miserably. No matter how much I slept, I still felt tired.

Not just "I need coffee" tired. Barely able to lift my arms to feed myself tired.

Finally, I realized that I couldn't make it through the day without an afternoon nap.

An afternoon nap? Even as a child, I did not nap. My endless energy was a perpetual nemesis to babysitters, playmates, brothers and mothers everywhere.

Memory loss. Weight gain. Fatigue. Naps?

Did I ask myself, "Wow, what's going on here?" No.

Did I take a day off work? No.

Did I call a doctor? No.

Did I continue my "fast forward" schedule? Yes!

It was like turning the page to the next chapter in my "make believe" health story. Except in my version of the fairy tale, the princess—me—does not get locked away in a castle alone to suffer. She develops a new super power. The ability to describe everything as "normal." Then, she starts believing in her own fairy tale.

Right now, you might be saying to yourself, "That's crazy! How could she ignore so many *obvious* signs? Why isn't she taking better care of herself?"

Except this isn't just my experience. My guess is you've experienced it, too. Something important you're ignoring. The thing that's *so obvious* to everyone around you.

What's trying to get your attention, right now, in a powerful way?

Is your partner treating you like crap, and everyone knows it but you? Did you agree to move back in because "it's going to be different this time?" Did you get bumped on your last promotion? Did you lose your job, or gain some weight? Maybe you are feeling unexplainably "down"—and maybe it's time to find some answers.

I believed I could outrun the demon that was chasing me. By running faster. Harder. Further. And, maybe you believe that, too.

So you run until you collapse. Only to get back up and keep running.

That's exactly what happened to me.

The only saving grace, in my case, was timing. During a routine annual exam, my doctor was checking my throat.

Nonchalantly, he said the four words you never ever want to hear:

What

is

this

lump?

A Lump? What?

"Yes, right here in your throat."

Aren't lumps bad? Do I have cancer?

I promise to sleep more. Exercise more. Eat less. Slow down. But. I. Can't. Be. *Sick*! I'm too busy! And I'm *way* too young!

Then came the dreaded words, "I would like to refer you for some further tests."

The check had finally bounced. The time had come. I could no longer ignore the symptoms. I couldn't run any faster. Or any further. Something was definitely wrong.

At that time, I had no idea how wrong.

Why does it take a crisis to force us to pause and prioritize?

After several sleepless nights and worry-filled days, it was time for my tests. I sat in the waiting room, fidgeting. I changed chairs. I moved back to the other chair. It didn't help.

The scans revealed a lump on my thyroid gland.

I was really sick. And all the willpower and accomplishments in the world couldn't make it better.

My only relief came from following the doctor's orders—a false hope that checking off a to-do list would put me back in control of an uncontrollable situation.

I was promptly referred to an endocrinologist.

This guy says that my problem is a simple one: Hashimoto's Hypothryoiditis. That was his diagnosis.

All I could think was, "Who is Hashimoto? And, why does he insist on coming to live with me without my permission?"

It was like hating a man I had never even met.

Besides being a mouthful, what is Hashimoto's Hypothryoiditis?

11

The Mayo Clinic says, "Hashimoto's is an autoimmune disorder in which your immune system attacks your thyroid gland. The thyroid gland is part of your endocrine system, which produces hormones that coordinate many of your body's activities."

To summarize, a man I don't know—Hashimoto—has decided to wage a war on my body.

From that point forward, I thought of Hashimoto as "The General." My internal organs were his willing army. And he was taking on new recruits daily.

My doctor was no match for The General. Because The General had an extensive strategy. My doctor had merely a single tactic: prescription medicine.

Medicine that I would need to take, and continue taking. For. Life.

For life?

Warm tears filled my eyes.

When he said the words, "No cure," I was devastated.

How could there be no cure?

You might be saying to yourself right now, "It doesn't sound that serious! Just take the medicine, and move on!"

I tried.

The medicine didn't work.

My lips turned blue.

My hair started falling out.

Swollen glands started protruding from my neck and from my head.

The more medicine I took, the worse I felt. Because the medicine was part of the problem. Except I didn't know that at the time.

When I was asked to take on more projects at work, I enthusiastically responded, "Yes!"

When I was invited to join not-for-profit boards, I enthusiastically responded, "Yes!"

I accepted every invite.

When people asked how I was doing, I cheerfully responded, "Great!"

Great?

(I'm not in a punk rock band, and I have blue lips! I'm shedding hair like a growing puppy and I walk on two legs! How is that great?)

"Great. More!"

Those two words became my stumbling blocks instead of my building blocks. Because I turned those two simple words into a captivating story I told myself repeatedly.

And for a two-word story, it was unbelievably powerful.

> You'll only be great when you do more!
> And you'll only be more when you appear great!

Have you ever told yourself a story like that? And then believed it?

That single story accelerated my downward spiral, because I refused to disconnect what I needed from what I thought everyone else needed of me.

I refused to prioritize my needs. In fact, I did just the opposite. I took on more than ever before.

Why?

Because I only knew one formula for success in life. And it had always worked. Success With More. (Maybe you're familiar with this formula? I first heard it from Brené Brown.)

Please + Perform + Perfect = Success With More

Be easy, pleasing and agreeable. Consistently exceed expectations. Appear to be perfect. Always take on more.

I tried to apply that formula to my health crisis. Do *exactly* what the doctor prescribes (that's the Please portion). Take on more responsibilities at work and in the community (Perform). Keep all commitments personally and professionally so as not to let anyone down (Perfect).

The problem? I couldn't solve my health crisis using the same formula that got me into the situation in the first place.

How often do you apply old formulas to solve new problems?

Even though I was following the doctor's orders. Even though I took each and every pill on time. Even though I kept working. Even though I kept volunteering. Even though I kept socializing. Even though I kept over achieving. Each blood test looked worse. Each day I felt worse. And crept closer toward looking how I actually felt.

Each day, it took more energy to make everything look "perfect."

One morning I looked in the mirror and literally did not know the exhausted person looking back at me.

Dull, grey, empty disks replaced my bright blue eyes. Thin, brittle hair had overtaken my long, full hair. Mysterious blotches, flecks and dry patches stole my previously clear complexion. Dull yellow skin had overtaken what was once porcelain. My face was littered with pencil thin red lines. I gained 30 pounds without having a baby.

I was so swollen, I looked like a basket of water balloons at a summer picnic.

Have you ever looked in the mirror and felt...shocked? Frozen? Ashamed?

I wanted to look away from the horrifying image. And to forever purge it from my mind.

All I could do was stare.

How. Did. I. Get... Here?

And how do I escape?

The calendar reminder on my phone rang out like an unexpected gunshot in broad daylight. No time for reflection!

I needed to get ready for a meeting.

The tipping point that morning was realizing I did not own a single piece of clothing that fit. All the shapewear in the world could not squeeze an extra-large body into a medium-sized suit.

I looked like a human tube of toothpaste, squeezed in the middle so tight that I threatened to burst forth at any moment.

I couldn't get ready. I collapsed on the floor in my closet and sobbed. Uncontrollably. Gasping for air. Inconsolable.

As I was choking just to breathe, I had a realization: who knew rock bottom felt like shag carpet?

I was tired. I was sick. I was fat. I was overwhelmed. I couldn't get up, physically or emotionally.

And, worst of all, I felt like a failure.

Do you know how it feels to hit rock bottom?

I always envisioned rock bottom as a literal low point. A line chart that looks like a "V." That after the "rock bottom moment," the climb toward the top begins again. The journey to redemption. Restoration. Triumph.

What I learned is that hitting rock bottom looks more like a "U." There's a low point that is then sustained over time. Connected to more low points.

Like walking through a scorching hot desert valley.

Without a drop of water. With nothing on the horizon except for more sand.

More heat.

More thirst.

What are you and I thirsting for in that moment?

Hope.

My thirst for hope at rock bottom became unquenchable. I was willing to take any test, try any pill or potion, see any specialist... *anything* that felt like a drop of water on the parched tongue of someone lost in an unrelenting desert.

As I scanned my horizon for hope, the picture was bleak. And getting worse.

New tests revealed my adrenal gland was now failing at the same rate as my thyroid. I was warned that other organs could follow.

Still no explanation. Only more pills.

Pills that didn't work.

And so another cycle began.

Needles. Scans. Tests. Referrals. Theories. Hope. Disappointment. Despair. Fear. Exhaustion.

Meanwhile, keep being pleasing! Keep performing at a high level, and appear to be perfect! Rinse and repeat.

The turning point came when my doctor finally admitted, "I don't know what's wrong with you. I don't know what else to do for you."

"But you're supposed to *help* me!," I reasoned. "I trusted you! And now you're abandoning me!"

I was alone. No one was coming to help me.

Did I cry? No.
Did I scream? No.
Did I threaten my Doctor? No.
Did I ask him any further questions? No.

Instead, I became totally numb. I had gone from feeling *everything* to feeling *nothing*.

What happened to that empty, dark, cold place inside? Emptiness covered me like a warm blanket on a cold day. My new normal was numbness—the source of new stories I told myself.

I wrapped myself in these feelings: "You'll never be healthy." "No one can help you." "Your situation is hopeless." "You brought this on yourself."

I resigned myself to my fate.

I would never reach the horizon of restored health. Ever.

My two-word story—*Great. More!*—became a one-word story. *Never*.

My quest for hope became a state of hopelessness.

And when you run out of hope, what happens next?

Do you quit? Withdraw? Collapse?

I experienced...an ending. For me, it was the ending of how I saw myself. I was no longer healthy. Vibrant. Energetic.

I now saw myself as weak. Broken. Incapable. Defeated. And far from invincible.

It wasn't until I came to the end of myself that I could begin to rely on others. To acknowledge that I needed help. Not help from confused doctors, who had little to offer, but help from the people around me who really cared.

It was a new beginning, and it started off like a scene from *A Christmas Carol*. I was visited by three uninvited guests, who shared conversations that shook to me to the core with their simplicity.

My Ghost of Christmas Past was a co-worker. He had successfully battled a myriad of health issues by taking a non-traditional treatment path.

My Ghost of Christmas Present was a friend who was currently battling a mysterious portfolio of symptoms. She was utterly frustrated, and she was pursuing a non-traditional path.

And my Ghost of Christmas Future was a college friend who just lost his mother. Having learned he shared the same genetic markers that she did—markers for the disease that had killed her—he was trying to fight heredity by pursuing a non-traditional path.

These three visitors saw my struggle and recognized it, because they were wandering through the same endless desert. They instinctively knew the signs.

"You look tired," Brian the Battle Warrior said.

"You look like you're really struggling," Amy the Anxious said.

"Is there anything I can do to help?" Larry the Loyal asked.

Their simple statements prompted me to open up about my struggle for the first time. I no longer had the energy to pretend I was "perfect." Or even "fine." Somehow describing my symptoms out loud made them feel more real. And the situation was more serious than I had been willing to admit.

What was it that made those three appearances...those conversations... such a revelation?

Three friends. Three conversations. One consistent simple recommendation.

"Let me refer you to my doctor. He practices holistic medicine, and he's transforming my health."

Wait. A holistic doctor?

I had visions of chanting. Voodoo. Woo-woo. Tofu. Eww!

(This is the upside of being a perpetual people pleaser: I agreed to call him. Only because I didn't want to let anyone down.)

Pulling into the parking lot for my first appointment felt like discovering a highly rated restaurant located in a strip mall. No matter how many amazing reviews you've read, you're still skeptical. So, just like you, I lowered my expectations. I simply didn't have the energy to be disappointed. Again.

Imagine my surprise when a perfectly normal looking person sat down across the desk from me. There was no incense. No Tarot cards. No request for my astrological sign. Just a trim, neatly dressed man with large, warm, brown caring eyes.

"How can I help you?" he inquired simply. His voice conveyed genuine warmth and interest.

I plopped a stack of paperwork on his desk with an emphatic thump.

Test results. Prescriptions. X-rays. Food diaries. Vital signs.

Then I described my long, treacherous, and exhausting journey through the desert called "Chronically Undiagnosed Illness."

After listening intently, he responded, "My goal is to understand the root cause of what's making you sick, not to prescribe medicine to treat your symptoms. The symptoms are just clues to the real problem."

Doesn't that sound so...simple? So...logical?

And yet...so unusual. It was, in fact, *the first time I heard those words from a medical professional.*

Then came the moment of truth, evaluating whether or not I wanted to have a second appointment and explore something new.

Even in my tired, sick, depressed, frustrated state, I knew one thing very clearly. The traditional path, the path I had been on, was leading me nowhere.

Have you ever stood at a crossroads in your life? Unsure of which way to go next? Or where that path will lead?

I stood at that same crossroads. Filled with uncertainty.

And, buried beneath my confusion, what was that? There was—could it be? A hint of...curiosity?

Desperation ultimately drove my decision to schedule a second date with the "hippie doctor." To take one more step down a new path. An alternate path.

What followed resembled the TV series, *House.*

You know the show. The central character in the series, Dr. Gregory House, uses unconventional techniques to solve medical mysteries. He leverages other medical experts plus his own experience and instincts to tirelessly pursue the correct diagnosis for each patient. He clashes with just about everything, ignoring traditional rules and methods.

Most importantly, he doesn't rest until his patients are cured.

My experience was similar. A tireless doctor in pursuit of a correct diagnosis...paired with a patient in deep decline.

At first, my new, alternate path seemed to mirror my previous, traditional path.

Needles. Scans. Tests. Referrals. Theories.

Hope. Disappointment. Despair. Fear. Exhaustion.

Except the tests were accompanied by a more thorough set of questions.

"Were you ever bitten by a dog?"

"Have your arms ever gone numb?"

"Have you ever found a tick on your skin?"

"Did you ever take these antibiotics?"

Soon I spent more time at the doctor's office than most people spend on Facebook. I inquired about a frequent guest rewards program. They gave me a magazine to read.

Progress looked different than I expected. Progress actually became finding more symptoms. Because each symptom provided another clue. Another insight to solving the great health mystery.

The latest symptoms included elevated liver enzymes. High estrogen. Low testosterone. Low adrenaline. Unusual red and white blood cell counts. Dangerously low mineral levels. Accompanied by an additional twelve-pound weight gain.

I expected a diagnosis. A cure. And *quickly*.

Meanwhile, my new favorite fabric? Stretchy. In any blend. A once tailored wardrobe transitioned to shapeless blobs filled with elastic. A bathing suit? Forget it! When cameras appeared at social gatherings, I disappeared faster than money at a mall.

Each test result felt like another data point in the rock bottom journey. Every visit to the doctor felt like a reinforcement of the stories I was telling myself. "You'll never be healthy." "Your situation is hopeless."

But strangely, I loved those doctor visits. Because each visit meant hope.

And then I hated those doctor visits, because needles were as prevalent as paperwork. I enjoyed the focused attention from a caring doctor. Then I hated him, for not being able to solve the mystery.

The collective effect of so much internal chaos eventually took its toll. Losing my health was the least of it. Poor health robbed me of the thing I loved most: my friends and family.

I didn't have enough energy to survive day to day. Much less spend time with the people I cared about. And when I did, it took days to recover.

Then came Karen's Last Stand. The battle with food.

First, a bit of context.

"Mangia," my last name, means, "Eat," in Italian.

> *It always seems impossible.*
> *Until it's done.*
> *- Nelson Mandela*

Our family events center on food. Some of my fondest memories involve special meals with special people. And I even completed a culinary degree for fun. Food was not just life. It was love.

Beyond that, I had been a vegetarian for 21 years. Which was more than a chosen lifestyle. It was a part of my identity.

Attending a business dinner? A night out with friends? I was *The Vegetarian.* A distinguishing label that was a differentiator. A title, of sorts.

So, imagine my surprise the day my doctor delivered an identity-altering prescription.

"Given what's happening with your body right now, you are no longer able to sustain your vegetarian lifestyle."

(Let me guess… Right now you're thinking one word: *Bacon.*)

I was also thinking one word: *No!*

And maybe a second word: *Way*!

Have you ever carried something old to a new place?

Maybe you just got a promotion, but you're still carrying the old story, "What if they find out I don't know what I'm doing?"

Or maybe you just started a new relationship, but you're still obsessing over, "What if this ends like the last one?"

Maybe you just moved to a new house or apartment. And took that old couch from college. The free one you found on the curb. Under the cover of night. With a hide-a-bed. And mauve flowers.

Just like that heavy, outdated couch, I was carrying my old success formula down my new path. And, because of it, each step forward became more treacherous.

Please + Perform + Perfect = Success With More

How long are you willing to carry heavy, old baggage to avoid confronting reality?

Why aren't you willing to leave it behind? To stop finding space for something that no longer fits? To make room for something new?

Not easy questions.

I was forced to release a label, a part of my identity—*The Vegetarian*. A label to which I assigned value.

You may have labels, too. Are you the overachiever? The introvert? The fixer? The peacemaker?

Are those labels moving you toward your ideal life? Helping you get there faster? Or holding you in place?

My doctor was the catalyst to release a label that no longer fit.

Because here's the harsh reality I encountered. (And, you will, too).

You can't take old labels with you to new places,
and expect to get different results.

You might be thinking, "The process of releasing old labels sounds painful! Why would I want to try when I'm comfortable right now?"

I'll tell you why:

The breakdown must come before the breakthrough.

After sobbing at the butcher shop counter (remember, 21 years and none of that beef stuff), I started researching Mayo Clinic admission criteria.

I was investigating a Leave of Absence from my job.

And then...

I got "The Call."

The woo-woo doctor with the kind eyes had found something.

The call I had been waiting for, for three and a half miserable years.

I sat alone in the doctor's office. Excited to see him. And dreading seeing him at the same time. What do I have? Is it terminal? Is there a treatment?

Calmly, the hippie doctor walked in and sat down to face me. His eyes looked at me so intently, I thought he was reading my soul.

He slowly tucked his long hair behind his right ear and paused. Silently, he opened the manila folder containing the results.

It was his turn to tell a two word-story. In a softly audible voice, he simply said, "Pesticide poisoning."

Wow. I did not see that coming.

I had so many questions. Yet couldn't seem to form them intelligently. I sat in shock.

How did this poisoning happen?

Hard to say with certainty, he assured me.

Is there a treatment plan? Fortunately, yes.

I felt grateful. Grateful for this alternate path. Grateful for hope restored. Grateful for this persistent, patient man who tirelessly pursued a correct diagnosis.

Treatment began one week later. I experienced some relief from my symptoms after just one treatment (mostly a reduction in fatigue).

Yet, there was still a long journey ahead.

In total, my journey from first signs of trouble to "cured" lasted almost eight years. Progress was slow at points. I experienced setbacks physically and emotionally, as you might imagine.

I wanted an overnight cure to a lifetime problem.

Can you relate?

As a child, pesticides had poisoned my body. As an adult, I had poisoned my own mind. A series of my long-held beliefs, labels, and stories became toxic over time. The lies looked like this:

- My good health will continue, no matter how I treat myself.
- I'll only be more when I accomplish more.
- Doing more and being more is the only formula for success.

What's your brand of personal poison?

Activity addiction? Self-limiting beliefs? Old stories? Not taking care of your health?

What happens on the inside eventually shows up on the outside. Just as it did for me.

The most important thing—the one event that started my cure—was taking time to pause—to pay attention to what I really needed. The foods, exercise and lifestyle changes evolved out of a pause that put me on the path that I'm on today.

A path with a revised formula for success:

Pause + Ponder + Prioritize = Success With Less

I'm so grateful to have come through this experience. And that I can share my experiences and what I've learned with you.

How does it feel to be cured after such a long battle? I am able to fully participate in my life. My career. My family. My community. And be energized by it, rather than drained by it.

Right now, you may find yourself facing a crossroads. Feeling confused and helpless. Let's take the first small step together, right now.

You are not alone. I've been there, too. And I'm with you there now—because you are reading this book for a reason.

To give you hope in your situation. To help guide you toward the healing that's inside all of us, if we just know where to look.

Choose one situation in your life to explore. It may be your physical health. Restoring a broken relationship. Or getting a promotion.

We'll apply the *Success With Less* formula to your circumstances, one step at a time.

To get past the breakdown.

And find the breakthrough.

3

Facing a Crossroads

When I'm facing a crossroads in my life, I look for signs. Ideally, those clear indicators of which path to choose. There's one sign I seek most consistently: the directional arrow that points to the path with no regrets.

Because I want to live my life with no regrets.

Don't you?

Living a life with no regrets is what *Success With Less* is all about.

Regrets are heavy baggage we carry in life. When we miss the school play for work. Fail in a relationship. Leave important words left unsaid. Let our priorities get way out of whack.

Regrets take up energy and space. They feel like bricks in a suitcase, constantly dragging behind you. Making the path to your next destination treacherous. Draining energy that could be used to enjoy the journey. Threatening to drag you to the ground at any moment. To that lowest, weakest, most powerless feeling version of yourself.

> *I never regret anything. Because every little detail of your life is what made you into who you are in the end.*
> *- Drew Barrymore*

I've been there.

I was engaged to be married. My lacy white dress hung in the closet, shining even in the shadows. Satin white shoes perched beside the dress.

The colors had been chosen. Invitations printed. Envelopes stamped. Bridesmaids invited. Deposits paid. Minister booked.

Only three milestones remained. My bridal shower. My college graduation. And my rehearsal dinner.

A thought quickly entered my mind, *Am I too young for this level of commitment?*

At first, it felt like I was adding pebbles to my suitcase of regrets. Little pebbles of doubt.

I would tell myself it was just nerves. Pre-wedding jitters. Completely normal. Everyone feels this way, right?

The thought returned, *Am I making the right decision? Am I ready for this?*

I'll never forget the day of my bridal shower. A dear friend had gone to an immense amount of trouble—sending invites, preparing dainty and delicious five-star-restaurant quality food.

Inside her home, there were beautiful decorations everywhere. Ladies dressed in pastels demurely sipped sherbet-laced punch. A pile of presents had grown into a department store holiday window display.

And my mom had made the four hour trip to be there.

The afternoon started out well enough. Laughter. Enjoyment. Stories. I felt light.

But as the afternoon progressed, I started to panic. With each gift I unwrapped, a heaviness developed in my stomach.

The giggles in the room sounded like a machine hum in my head. The smile on my face began to freeze—fixed so tight my face might crack. I could hear the sound of my own pulse in my ears.

The mounting pile of gifted housewares looked more like an anchor than a harbor. And one thought kept going through my head.

I can't go through with this wedding.

Paranoid that the ladies in the room could hear the thoughts in my head, I broke out in occasional nervous laughter. But the giggles weren't me—I was watching myself from across the room. Who was this strange person? She looked like me. She was the guest of honor. But she was no longer there. Instead she was lost in a sea of panicked thoughts.

The drive back to my apartment with my mom was a quiet one. I alternated between nausea and tears, because I was rehearsing a conversation in my head I wasn't sure I was ready to have out loud.

You know what I wanted to say. What I wanted to do.

It wasn't quite that easy.

Because my fiancé was living with my parents at the time.

And after the wedding? We both had full-ride scholarships to get our Masters' degrees. At the same university. In the same program. In a small town. While living with one of his relatives.

This wasn't *just* a wedding. It wasn't *just* the money. The decision to get married or not would literally affect every area of my life.

No wedding meant no job. No scholarship. No place to live.

I had no "Plan B."

How was the student graduating with honors suddenly without a plan? Shouldn't I have been smart enough to think through whether or not to get married sooner?

I was standing at a crossroads. And I could only see one path. The traditional path: graduate, get married. Keep your commitments. Don't let anyone down.

When you're standing at a critical crossroads, what do you do next?

Pause.

Why pause? Especially when your brain is telling you to slam the accelerator to the floor?

When all you want to do is race away from that vastly uncomfortable moment of indecision as quickly as possible.

Pause.

Because that speed-demon moment might cause you to miss valuable road signs—signs that tell you when it's time to exit.

In my case, my desired destination was living a life with no regrets. Could I find the exit?

Because marrying the wrong person seemed like a life filled with regrets.

Regrets compel us to look in the rear view mirror. To revisit. To doubt. To question ourselves and our judgment. To live in the past.

> And there are only two ways to view your life:
> through the rear view mirror or through the windshield.

Looking back. Or looking ahead.

When you're looking in the rear view mirror, how much more likely are you to crash?

If taking a pause is beneficial in avoiding a crash, why are we all—myself included—tempted to skip this step?

- Pausing is uncomfortable. After the wedding shower, when I was alone in the car with my mom and with my thoughts, I was terrified. No polite ladies' laughter to drown out the voices in my head. Nothing to distract me from the difficult decision I needed to make. I didn't know what to do next. I wanted to go through with the wedding just to get away from my own thoughts.

- You don't recognize you've reached a crossroads. I had been at a crossroads for months. I just didn't realize it. I had competing priorities, like making wedding plans, sending out graduation invitations, you name it. The crossroads was already crowded with other people, so I didn't notice my location. All I saw was: graduate, get married. I thought I was on the same long, straight, narrow path as everyone around me. There didn't appear to be a crossroads. Or a reason to hit the brakes.

- No decision is an easier decision. No evaluation required. No messy trade-offs or emotions. It's easy for you and me to let a series of small decisions ultimately become the big decisions. At least in the short-term. In my case, attend the bridal shower that's already on the calendar. And keep checking wedding tasks off my to-do list.

- Pressure from others. You and I want to be liked and to be loved. To belong. I believed everyone around me wanted me to get married. I found it difficult, and maybe you do, too, to differentiate pressure from within myself with pressure from others. Wanting to please other people with your choices is a normal feeling. And how your choices affect the people you care about most is an important consideration when making a big decision. But remember: what other people need and want *can't be the only factor in your decision.* Consider this: Do your friends want you to live a happy, fulfilled life? Does your family want you to live a happy, fulfilled life? The answer is likely yes. The pressure about how to live that life is pressure you and I put on ourselves. In the case of my wedding, I realized I was the only one who would live in the marriage day to day...which meant the other votes no longer counted. The pressure you feel to please others and to please yourself can be reconciled by articulating how the choice you are making enables you to live your best life.

- Saying yes feels easier. Be easy, be agreeable, be likeable. Just say yes and follow the crowd. If the path is already crowded, it must be the best path, right? *Wrong.*

- Ego factor. I wanted to be seen as "having it all together." Marriage. Scholarship. Education. "Success!" I wanted other people to see me as successful, not as a runaway bride with a dead-end job who's playing beneath her potential. Maybe you've been there, too, taking the man, or the job, or the courses, in spite of what your heart tells you. Is it really worth it to live in debt, just to have the best-dressed kids or the biggest house? Worth it to whom, exactly?

- Perceived impact to time and resources. I knew I was literally running out of time. The wedding was 60 days away. And if I also turned down the scholarship, I literally had no way to financially support myself. I could not see a solution to my time and resource issues in the panic of making a decision. The pause is the antidote to panic...if you can find it.

- You don't know what you want. It's like being hungry without knowing what you're hungry for. Sometimes you and I know what we're doing isn't working. And dwelling on that thought is draining. Depressing. Overwhelming. Especially if the pressure to make a decision feels urgent. I knew I didn't want to get married, but I honestly didn't know what I wanted instead.

My pause lasted as long as the car ride to my apartment. From what I recall, the longest 17 minutes of my life.

My mom parked the car and started to pop the trunk so we could carry the gifts inside. As we walked around to the back of the car, I started to cry. I couldn't stop the sentence that was going to change my life.

"Mom, I can't go through with the wedding."

Followed by, "Don't unload the gifts." (I was upset, but I was also practical).

She was very quiet. Silently, we walked up the stairs to my second-story apartment.

In the hours that followed, I called off my engagement. Burned through an entire box of Kleenex. And returned every single gift. The guests were in shock.

And, I guess, so was I.

Staring directly into the eyes of each bridal shower attendee while handing back still-boxed gifts was absolutely brutal. Especially when accompanied by their looks of confusion. Sadness. Horror. Disappointment.

But as brutal as those conversations were,
that 17-minute pause saved me from a lifetime of regrets.

From dragging a heavy suitcase behind me. From looking in the rearview mirror. From always wondering, "What if?"

Even though I knew calling off the wedding was my path to a life of no regrets, I was sad. Ashamed. I was disappointed in myself. My vision for my life would not come to be...at least not in the way I envisioned it.

You might not be calling off an engagement. Or turning down a scholarship. But every day you are making important decisions, wondering about your relationships, and thinking, "This doesn't feel right!"

How do you know if you're facing a crossroads in your life? You might notice these signs:

- You are presented with a new opportunity or idea (and you find it intriguing)
- A long-held dream begins to consistently resurface (open a business, travel the world, go back to school)
- You've experienced a significant loss or setback (job, relationship, health)
- The way you've succeeded in the past is no longer producing results
- People and experiences that previously brought you joy and happiness now feel empty and unfulfilling
- You're going through the motions and you no longer know why
- You're asking yourself, "Is this all there is to look forward to?"

- You're overwhelmed with the desire to abandon something that previously held deep meaning to you (job title, career climb, material possessions, significant relationship)

When you face a crossroads, when you feel uncertain, when your path forward is unclear: Pausing is a source of power.

Pressing the pause button on the activity level in your life temporarily quiets the chaos around you, so you can hear your own voice.

And you won't be able to trust your gut in your crossroads situation until you are quiet enough to hear your own voice. Your own intentions. Your own fears.

Whether your pause lasts 17 minutes in the car—like mine did—or takes place across weeks and months, use your powerful pause to ask yourself one question:

Why?

- Why am I feeling conflicted about my current situation?
- Why have my feelings about my current situation changed?
- Why have I postponed making a decision about my current situation?
- Why am I afraid to make a change?
- Why am I optimistic about making a change?
- Why have I not pursued an alternate path before?

When you pause to evaluate your feelings and your options, you put distance between your current situation and the decision you need to make.

The distance between chaos and calm is a powerful pause.

Sometimes the distance you need between you and your crossroads is emotional. Sometimes the distance you need between you and your crossroads is physical.

I'll never forget the one phone call that lingered on my to-do list after calling off my engagement: the call to my travel agent.

"I need to cancel my honeymoon trip," I postured with confidence I didn't feel, "and use the funds for a trip with my girlfriends instead. And, yes, you heard me correctly."

Stunned silence. Followed by the sound of her fingers clicking away on the keyboard.

Even though I paused long enough to make two critical decisions at my crossroads—end my engagement and turn down my graduate assistantship—I was still not clear on a path forward. I had kicked up so much dust with those two decisions, I couldn't see through my own emotional haze.

Physical distance would help me gain emotional distance. And also create breathing room for other options—options I couldn't see when I was too close to my situation—to surface.

When the airplane lifted off the ground a few weeks later, I watched my problems temporarily fade away as I left the city behind. My only job at that point was to look forward. To pause and look for new road signs along the way. To gain perspective.

> *I will never regret you or say that I wish I had never met you. Because, once upon a time, you were exactly what I needed.*
> *- Anonymous*

During my pause, I surrounded myself with people who were invested in me. Not in my situation. Between sleeping and sightseeing, I was surrounded with support. My two girlfriends intermittently listened. Offered advice. And helped me think through options.

What I learned from putting distance between me and my situation is that pausing is a great time to:

35

- Evaluate possible alternatives. What paths do you see? Where might each path lead you? Which paths take you closer to achieving your goals? Take time to consider your options—all of them, no matter how far-fetched. That's the power of the pause. Don't waste it.

- Look for road signs. Scan the environment around you. Look for clues. Get curious. Where might unexpected signs—like a new relationship, a job offer, or vacation—lead you next? Could any of your possible paths intersect? For example, would going back to school enable you to pursue a job that's always been of interest?

- Set guard rails. Otherwise known as boundaries or guidelines, these are the "must haves" versus the "nice to haves" in your situation. When you are clear about what matters most, you create criteria through which to evaluate your options.

- Ask for directions. Others around you may have stood at a similar crossroads. Ask for input. Asking for directions is the hardest one for me. And it might be difficult for you, too. What I've learned is that I would rather ask for help than to fail. Asking for help is easier for me when I have a network of people I trust, because we already have a relationship. And they know me outside of my crisis situations. Who do you know and trust that can help in your crossroads moments? What are you afraid to give up, if it means you will gain a helping hand?

- Map out your destination. Redefine success. Throw out the old map. And the old directions. Your destination may have changed—you better get comfortable with a new route. Who could help you define your new destination and navigate new roads to get there?

- Unpack your suitcase. Unload the damaging stories you are telling yourself. The limiting labels you assign to yourself. Like regrets, self-limiting stories are heavy baggage. Just like you, I'm tempted to listen to the stories in my head. "You can't do this." "You'll never figure this out. "You've failed at this before." Lighten your load by pausing these stories. Think of examples where those stories are wrong. Because they are. Because you are more than your past. Because you can let go of the baggage as soon as you decide to do so.

Your crossroads moment is an opportunity to discover your potential. You can simplify what's in your suitcase. You can lighten your load, and make room for new experiences. New people. New success.

With no regrets.

And that's exactly what happened to me.

While I was traveling, one of my mentors saw something I never could have seen on my own.

When I returned from Vacationland, she called to share the breakthrough in my situation.

"I know you're in a time of transition," she empathized, "and uncertain about what to do next. While you were traveling, one of your friends resigned his all-expenses paid graduate assistantship because he has a limited time opportunity to play professional volleyball. Which means I now have space for you in my Masters' program. Print out your resume. Put on a suit. And come meet with the Director of the program today."

Someone else's pause became my payoff.

I followed a new path that day. A path that was hidden, until I took a pause. A path I would not have been ready to pursue until I put distance between my crisis and my crossroads.

When I was offered the all-expenses paid graduate assistantship to earn my Masters' degree a week later, I enthusiastically accepted. One step at a time, I was moving toward a better life than I ever dreamed possible.

With no regrets.

And that's what *Success With Less* is all about. A no-regrets approach to life.

4

The Formula For *Success With Less* Explained

I had just been assigned to a high-stakes, highly visible, highly urgent project at work. An 18-month project was condensed to eight months. With no budget and no resources, we had no chance of success.

Have you ever been assigned to a project like that?

My job was to work with my colleague to deliver in full and on time. *No matter what.*

Unfortunately, I took that statement literally.

Imagine nervous executives in a politically-charged environment. They're never satisfied and always paranoid. Overworked, exhausted, de-motivated employees couldn't care less.

And the firm knowledge that your next promotion was on the line.

I was standing at a career crossroads. And I was faced with the same two options you have when you're presented with a new opportunity.

Invest, or divest?

Proceed forward? Turn back?

Or find a new path?

Earning a promotion was important to me. I had been working toward it for years.

I invested.

Not only did I invest, I over-invested. Nights. Middle of the nights. Weekdays. Weekends. No hour was too late. Or too early.

I ran full-speed into a burning blaze of activity every single day, without hesitation.

But I overlooked one important safety procedure.

Divest.

When you invest in something new, you must divest of something else. I'm not talking about divesting from your career, and investing in knitting. I'm talking about a simple give-and-take decision that happens in small increments, not radical life-changing decisions. In other words, the kinds of decisions you make every day.

When I chose to invest in the high-stakes project at work, I failed to divest of any of my other responsibilities.

What could possibly go wrong?

When you fail to divest before you invest, you lay the foundation on which to build damaging stories. And habits. "I have to keep all the plates spinning!" "I'm sure I can do it all if I just try a little harder!" "I don't want to be seen as a quitter!" "I'm so busy that I must be important! And successful!"

While I was fully invested in the high-stakes project, I tried to keep all the plates spinning in my life. Hosting dinner parties. Volunteering. Maintaining family time.

I was burning with so much activity that I was quickly getting burned out myself.

Have you put yourself in that position before?

By the time we delivered our project, I was exhausted, irritable and miserable. Even worse, I made people around me miserable, with my constant "Poor me" stories.

But I kept telling myself, "We succeeded! And there are no asterisks next to success!"

Or are there?

My personal pep talk was interrupted as my cell phone buzzed like a live animal in my purse. It was my boss. Ten minutes before holiday break, and he was about to change the entire course of my new year.

In a whisper, he asked, "Are you in a place where we can talk?"

Uh-oh.

Maybe our project wasn't successful.

"Congratulations! You've been promoted!" he cheered.

I stifled the impulse to cry. My "thank you" was barely audible. I had a burning fever. No voice. Sinus congestion. Itchy eyes. Fatigue. My chest so heavy I felt like I was hosting a disco dance party for energetic elephants. All symptoms I had ignored for over a week, due to being too busy to go to the doctor.

I was too sick to enjoy what I had sacrificed my health to achieve.

Success felt more like a setback. I gained a promotion. I lost my perspective.

I was willing to invest in my career at the cost of divesting in my health, my wellness, my family, and my friends.

I was left with one nagging question. "Was spending the extra time at work really worth what it cost me?"

The next morning, I sequestered myself on the couch. Instead of sipping champagne, I sipped cold medicine. Straight from the bottle. While mindless game shows buzzed in the background, guilty reminders buzzed through my head:

- *"Do you remember how sick you became the last time you chose your work over your health?"*
- *"Didn't you learn anything from your health crisis?"*
- *"How many times do you have to learn the same lesson about priorities?"*

As the discarded tissue pile overflowed the trash can, I paused.

It was New Year's Eve.

"I will resolve that I will find a new way to succeed next year. And that I will redefine success on my terms."

Little did I know at the time, my boss had the same goal for me.

Months later, an early morning coffee stop gave me the jolt I needed. And it wasn't from the caffeine.

I stopped to pick up coffee on the way to an all-day meeting—the kind of meeting you see on your calendar and think, "Again? Didn't we just have one of these?"

As I marched into the coffee shop, I noticed my boss' boss.

"I'll wait in line with you," he said.

Wow, I thought. A whole day together ahead of us, and yet you and I get to make small talk now. Lucky me.

"Have you thought about what you want to do next in your career?" he said.

I didn't want conversation. I just wanted coffee and a quick exit.

What? Are we really going to do this *here*? In line. For coffee. In the morning rush?

It was the drive-by career coaching session of my nightmares. It was my very own Little Coffee Shop of Horrors.

My next sentence sounded like something from a corporate comic strip. I think I said, "Continue to build my business acumen...Uh... Grow into the promotion I've just received...Team player...Umm... Learn from you...Find a mentor...Synergy..." (and other corporate stuff that I thought was important).

Do you ever stumble when you have the opportunity to take a big step?

The executive did not blink. His piercing stares only accelerated my runaway verbal train.

A lesser executive might have written me off entirely at that point.

Instead, he offered to help. Which, somehow, felt worse.

"I am going to connect you with my executive coach," he emphatically stated. "She'll help get you on the right path. You can't continue going at this same pace and have any promotions left in your future."

Did I thank him? No. Did I ask him about the executive coach? No.

Instead I responded, "Okay," through gritted teeth. My jaw was clenched. All the while thinking, *If only I had been able to answer his career question...I wouldn't have to endure the certain torture and total waste of time that is to follow.*

How often do you turn down help when you need it most? Even when it's being offered by someone who's invested in your success?

Why do you insist on trudging on alone?

The only reason I budged from that career-crossroads moment was because I was being pushed. Against my will. With my future career held hostage.

So I didn't even contact the executive coach.

I hoped she wouldn't contact me.

You know where I'm going with this.

She called me. Of course she did!

I was gracious and engaging.

No, I wasn't. I was furious.

I was "surface-level compliant." Exchanging pleasantries. Inquiring about the process. Appearing to be agreeable.

The same belligerent acceptance you offer those trying to help you when you don't want to be helped. Or don't think you need to be helped.

> *It's what you learn after you know it all that counts.*
> *- Earl Weaver*

On the surface, her formula looked familiar. She would gather feedback from my bosses, my employees, and my peers. She would share the results. We would build a plan based on the feedback.

Fine. Except it really wasn't.

Let's just get this over with—quickly and painlessly. I do *not* have time for *this*!

I'll never forget the afternoon I sat down with her to hear the results of her research. We were sitting outside on a screened in porch. Facing each other across the table. The sound of a neighbor's yard being mowed faintly in the background. The smell of freshly cut grass wafting through the air.

I had no idea I was about to be mowed down to size also.

She started by explaining the process. How she gathered the feedback.

Blah, blah, blah.

Then she started in with both guns blazing. Detailing the strengths I'd heard many times before. And then introducing a phrase that was new to me. "Strength Overused."

What does that even mean?

It means that any strength taken to excess becomes a weakness.

You may be positive, energetic and encouraging. When you behave that way in the face of disaster, you may be viewed as naïve. Disconnected. Disingenuous.

You may be analytical, fact-driven, and avoid risk. When you behave that way in the face of an opportunity, you may be viewed as slow. Unable to make a decision. Lagging.

You may be improvisational, highly adaptable, and willing to change course at a moment's notice. When you behave that way in the face of a major deliverable, you may be viewed as flighty. Lacking a clear direction. Unable to get things done.

"When you are under pressure to deliver," she said, "you come across as being willing to win at the cost of your health, your colleagues, and your life balance. When you behave that way as a leader, you send an unintended signal that you expect the people around you to win at all cost as well. And that is not the kind of leader your boss is seeking."

Pregnant pause.

Simply put, what got me to the point of my promotion—investing without divesting—was not going to take me any further. And might actually end up costing me my job.

How do you react when you're confronted with less than flattering feedback?

I've heard the saying many times, "Feedback is a gift."

Well, in that moment, I was looking for the return receipt. Because I didn't want to accept the gift.

I let her drone on until I could no longer hear her voice over my own need to defend myself.

> Have you ever defended yourself to someone
> offering you wise counsel?

It never crossed my mind that her observations might be legitimate. Especially given that the observations resulted from the sum of numerous conversations with people I interacted with daily.

I matched her voice in tone and in volume. Daring her with my eyes to even try to interrupt my swelling tidal wave of fury.

Without a single breath it all came out of me. "You don't understand the pressure I was under to deliver! I got the job done and no one quit, so how could the situation possibly be this dire? I'm sorry that my weekend emails were inconvenient, but someone had to be in charge!"

And, then when I had really lost all self-control, "Is this because I'm female?"

Oh. You. Didn't!

Yes. I. Did.

Sometimes you and I use our labels as our excuses.

> My circumstances had nothing to do with my gender.
> And everything to do with my choices.

That's how desperate I was to make my issues someone else's fault. That's how uncomfortable I was sitting with the thought that I wasn't perfect. That's how much I wanted to prove that change was beyond my control. And unnecessary.

Because I felt attacked. Uncomfortable. Exposed. Vulnerable. Afraid. Disappointed. Not just in the feedback itself. But in how I reacted to it.

Have you ever felt that way? I call it "Blamestorming."

In a final grasp at salvaging our session and my self-dignity, I said, "Fine!" (There's that word again!) "Just give me the formula or the framework, and next time we can pick an area to apply it."

A lifetime of behaviors and patterns. And I asked her for a formula. A quick fix. The equivalent of a weekend home improvement project when my house had been crumbling at the foundation for years.

What foundational behaviors are threatening to sink you?

Like me, maybe it's your need to make progress at the cost of your relationships, your health, and your quality of life. Maybe you're living in the past. Revisiting old hurts and letting them control you. Or failing to take accountability.

Remember:

The break*down* must come before the break*through*.

That conversation with my executive coach prompted my breakdown. I left with a long list of books to read and videos to watch, which I referred to my friends as, "You're A Circus! Embrace Your Inner Clown!"

The assignment? We would meet every week for six months. That's right. Imagine anticipating a conversation like that. Every. Single. Week. And the only topic on the agenda is *you*.

The only reason I read the books and watched the videos was because I wanted to check the box. To be relentlessly pleasant. Agreeable. And to have her report back that I was a good student. Even her best student.

I still wasn't motivated to make changes. Even in the face of all of that feedback.

How often do you treat the most important
conversations in your life as a check-the-box exercise?

I've been guilty of that many times. Say what you think people want to hear. Then move on. Just tuck your thoughts and feelings a little deeper inside. Or dismiss them completely. Don't rock the boat.

The improvement project was me. The new formula for success to invent was my own. And I was faced with the same two options you and I discussed earlier. Invest in the self-improvement project. Or divest in the self-improvement project. At the cost of my career.

This time when I chose to invest, I divested other meetings on my calendar. To make room for the breakthroughs that were to come.

In a subsequent conversation, my executive coach inquired, "Do you know why I want you to read these books?" referring to the assigned materials on feelings and behaviors.

"Not really," I responded.

"You are spending all of your energy focused on the *what*. I'm here to help you understand *why*," she explained.

Huh?

I wanted to focus on "what is the behavior" and how to mask it. To diminish it. To shift it slightly. To make the behavior less of a burden on others. She was focused on the much bigger prize called "why do you have this behavior?"

That's much more personal! And much more difficult to unravel.

Because your underlying behaviors and habits don't just show up at work. They show up at home, too. In your personal relationships. In your finances. In where you spend your time. And with whom you spend your time.

When you are standing at a crossroads, it's not just about what you're going to do next. It's about why you do or don't want to take a particular path.

I had never been confronted with that reality in such simple terms.

The behaviors that were holding me back at work were also holding me back in life.

How had I not connected that before?

Throughout the course of numerous sessions. Painful conversations. Confronting reality. Many books. Even more videos. I arrived at the first version of my new formula for success. The behaviors I needed to translate into habits, personally and professionally.

As a result, I wrote three words on a sticky note. And stuck the note to my laptop to keep me focused. The three words were:

Pause.

Ponder.

Ask.

Why those three words? Why those specific behaviors?

Pause
I was guilty of being in constant motion. Doing without thinking. Jumping before looking. Racing to the finish line without considering whether the race needed to be finished, or even if anyone else needed to be in the race with me. Maybe you can relate. Because of that, I learned I needed to pause:

- The first responder, in every situation. The one who talks first, responds to the email first, and comes to the rescue first. That was me. Why? Because when I acted as the first responder, I didn't leave room for anyone else to participate. I was missing valuable context that would have prompted a different reaction or course of action. First responder mode was an exhausting way to live.
- My activity level. My calendar was back-to-back every day, all day, seven days a week. Sometimes with overlapping commitments in the same time slot. Pausing to evaluate what

was on my calendar instead of just taking the next meeting gave me time to think through why the meeting was on my calendar, and whether or not the meeting needed to be there. I wore activity as my primary badge of "success." Have you ever equated "busy" with "accomplished?"

- The stories in my head. You and I tell ourselves stories constantly. The stories we play on a constant reel tend to include phrases like, "I can't..." "I'll never..." and "I should." When I put the stories in my head on pause, I was more open to trying new approaches to solving old problems. And to redefining the true measure of success.

Ponder

When I'm busy doing, I'm rarely thinking. I'm just trying to survive. When I made progress on pressing pause, I used the time to consider:

- Does this need to be done right now? Why does it need to be done right now? What happens if it doesn't get done right now? What are the consequences? I learned that when I am overscheduled, everything seems urgent. Even when it's not. Because I could no longer tell the difference. I just knew I had a limited amount of time, and if something was going to get done, it needed to get done NOW. There was no later.

- Do I need to be the one to do it? "If you want the job done right, then do it yourself." A liar said that. Nothing could be further from the truth. Look at the meetings on your calendar. Do you have to attend? If you have an employee who is ready for more visibility, ask her to attend instead. At home, make a list of chores. Then get everyone in your household to sign up for something. Consider what you can hire someone to do (i.e., mow the grass, shovel the snow, iron the clothes).

- What happens if I do something else instead? Where else could I spend my time and energy?

Ask

Get curious. Inquire further. Explore other options, possibilities and resources.

Clarifying questions. When I first implemented my *Pause + Ponder + Ask* framework, something interesting happened. I would be part of a conversation and, instead of responding, I would *listen*.

Then, instead of making a statement, I would ask a question. Questions fixed a lingering problem from my past: because I was often missing a key fact, insight or nuance, my initial reaction was incorrect. Asking questions is also a powerful tool for engaging others, by making space for their expertise and insights.

- For input. While you're in the mode of asking questions, consider using a few of these: "How have you handled a similar situation in the past?" "I need to make a decision about which project to pursue, do you have any thoughts?" "I'm stuck, do you have any ideas?" When you ask, others will gladly share their thoughts.
- The "What If" question. In a contentious situation with competing agendas, I've found this question helps. "What if we incorporated both of your ideas into the plan to our boss?" Here's another version. "What if you pick up the kids after work, and I drop them off before work?" "What if we don't finish the project on time?" The "what if" question allows everyone to participate and to negotiate a path forward without having to own a bold or controversial statement.

Pause. Ponder. Ask.

Those three words became permanent prompts to change my behavior. And, over time, I modified those three words slightly to create the *Success With Less* formula:

Pause + Ponder + Prioritize = Success With Less

What I learned is that asking questions is a foundational concept. So, I replaced "ask" with "prioritize."

Why?

Because after you pause to think, you will need to make choices. When I take the time to pause and to ponder, it's easier to arrive at a clear list of priorities. And to stick with them.

Why is *Success With Less* a winning formula at work and in life? I've learned that the *Success With Less* formula makes it easier for me to say "no." With less guilt. Less emotion. And to stay on my path to a life with no regrets.

Here's an example. I was offered a promotion. The promotion meant relocating to another town where I did not have family, friends, or a network of colleagues. I paused to consider the opportunity. I didn't try to make a decision during my busiest day of the week. I pondered what would happen if I took the job...and if I didn't take the job. Ultimately, I prioritized that staying close to my family was most important.

Which made it easy to say no. And the conversation went like this. "Thank you for the opportunity to consider this great promotion. I took some time to think about it. Spending time with my family here in town is a higher priority to me right now than accepting this new role. If my priorities change, I'll let you know."

Here's a secret. It's very difficult for people to argue with your priorities. Especially where family is involved. In fact, most people will congratulate you for clearly defining your priorities.

Right now you might be thinking, "Great! I want to be on a path to a life with no regrets! I'm ready to take on the *Success With Less* formula! And apply it to every aspect of my life!"

Perhaps we should press pause on radical reinvention?

You need to start small. With a series of building blocks.

Which reminds me of a time when I tried to take on too big of a goal too soon.

While training with a friend for a half-marathon, I let him convince me that we should sign up for a triathlon. "After all, we're already in shape from training for the half marathon."

I should have listened to my gut. I didn't.

Instead, I went online and registered for my first Sprint triathlon, which consisted of a 750-meter swim, a 20K bike ride, and a 5K run.

Training for a triathlon with the support of athletic friends sounds like a great and reasonable goal...until you examine the facts. We signed up for the triathlon just *eight short weeks in advance*. There were only six weeks between the half marathon and the triathlon.

Oh, and I had never swum a lap before in my life.

Plus the only bike I owned was the mountain bike I inherited from my brother when he graduated college.

And this wasn't just any bike. It was the "Black Beast." A hunk of metal so heavy, with tires so wide, it looked like it belonged on the free weight rack at a local gym.

When the Black Beast and I went out on our first date, I realized we might not be destined to become soulmates. A seat so hard, gears so grinding, that I wondered if it was time for us to start seeing other people.

Do you know that saying about learning to ride a bike? Well, it's not true. Not all of us remember.

Given these factors, any reasonable person would have delayed for a later race. By contrast, I fully embraced my "success" formula at the time:

Please + Perform + Perfect = Success With More

It went something like this:

- Please: I want to please my friend. Backing out would let him down and I don't want to do that!

- Perform: No matter how many items are on your to-do list, you *should* be able to handle just one more.
- Perfect: If you back out now, everyone will finally have the confirmation they need once and for all to prove that you're "not successful." Or perfect.

Triathlon day will live forever in my memory. The Black Beast and I arrived early to check in, and I was tattooed with a black Sharpie marker.

Unfortunately, one small detail had escaped my preparation. In my mind, the sequence of events would be run-bike-swim. After all, doesn't it make sense to have a refreshing "water cool down" as the final event?

In actuality, the sequence of events was swim-bike-run. Since swimming was my worst event, that meant draining the best of my energy right from the start.

> How often do you use your best energy
> toward activities with the least return?

Yes, I finished the triathlon. Barely. Mostly because the last part of the run was downhill, so I could have literally rolled to the finish line. The only record broken that day was my own for most outlandish number of difficult tasks in a single weekend.

> Why do you set marathon goals
> when a walk around the block is your current fitness level?

A reasonable goal, given my fitness level, would have been to run a 5K or to bike a 20K.

Maybe swim half a K. (Would that be an "O-K?")

Trying to take on too many big development goals at the same time left me feeling more failed and exhausted than successful and energized.

54

Do you feel overwhelmed and discouraged
when you try to make too many changes at once?

Whether you're training for an actual triathlon, trying to balance life's perpetual triathlon (Family—Career—Health, where all events happen all at once), or implementing the *Success With Less* formula in your life, don't go too far too fast. The key is setting your goals in small, realistic increments, based on your level of fitness *right now*.

If you're an activity addict, always on the go, exiting all of your commitments simultaneously is daunting. The transition from Tasmanian Devil to a balanced calendar and life is not a single step.

That's why you and I are going to apply the *Success With Less* formula one step at a time to key aspects of your life. Your calendar. Your career. Your relationship. Your health.

As you learn to apply the *Success With Less* formula, it will feel like learning to ride a bike again.

You may feel rusty, imbalanced, and unsure.

I did.

And if you fall off the bike the first time? Or the second time? No one dies. You're still here. You've survived worse.

Just like a triathlon is completed one step, one pedal, one stroke at a time, freeing yourself from constant activity happens one minute, one meeting, one moment at a time.

5

Success With Less in Your Calendar

Think about your checking account. You likely get paid once or twice a month. Which means every two weeks you have a limited amount of money to align to your priorities. To take care of your needs.

When you and I have limited resources, our priorities tend to rise to the top. Rent. Mortgage. Utilities. Food. Transportation.

Why? Because you and I immediately see the link between the investment and the return. Or at least have a clear understanding of the consequences. No rent payment? Nowhere to live. No utility payments? No running water or electricity.

You know the consequences of spending funds in your checking account. If you've spent years paying on a student loan or a large credit card balance, you know that debt—paying today for what you experienced yesterday—takes a significant toll. Adds stress. And often leads to regrets. Debt also constrains your ability to participate in and enjoy future experiences.

What does this have to do with your calendar?

Like your paycheck, each day 24 hours are deposited into your calendar balance. Each day you and I are faced with a choice about how to align limited time resources with our biggest priorities. So, why do you and I allocate the bulk of the balance to the areas of least return? And how often do we saddle ourselves with calendar debt by committing beyond what we reasonably have to give?

You and I frequently do the opposite with our time than we do with our money.

"But, I'm great at managing my time," you might say! "And I'm doing what I have to do to survive right now!"

So am I. But when I pause to review the way I'm spending my limited calendar balance, I'm left with one overarching thought.

Your schedule is full, your soul is empty.

Can you relate?

Consider the precious 24 hours you and I have each day.

What would happen if you treated those 24 hours as 24 gifts?

Gifts that you could give to whoever you choose, even to yourself.

When I looked at my calendar, I observed I was willingly giving the precious gift of my limited time to everyone who asked. And, with only 24 gifts to give each day, I was writing the biggest checks to work. And the smallest checks to myself.

Does your calendar look that way, too?

One of the money management principles I learned from my parents was, "Pay yourself first."

Have you heard that? It's the idea that you should put money in a savings account or a retirement account before paying your daily bills. And before fringe or fun spending.

Do you pay yourself first, on your calendar?

Do you take care of your most important relationships and your health now as an investment in your long-term future?

"My relationships are going great, thank you," you might be saying. "I just went to my kid's ballgame last night! I'm even the assistant coach. I have this under control!"

Do you?

My guess is that someone meaningful in your life is trying to get your attention right now in a powerful way.

Maybe not by screaming or by begging. Maybe it's a slow drift.

Maybe it's been a long time between deposits of your best time and energy—there's been too much time between gifts. For example, you might have missed date night together for the past six weeks...or months. Your child wants you to come outside and play, but you're always working. Or on your phone.

You never quite find the time on your calendar.

Here's the dilemma we face:

> If you and I are only given the gifts of limited time and money,
> how do we put both to work for us? Thinking of time like an
> investment, how can we generate the greatest returns?

I'll never forget the call I received from Amy, a long-time colleague turned dear friend. She's the friend who remembers your birthday, and knows how you're feeling without you needing to say.

My birthday was quickly approaching, and Amy could have chosen to purchase an expensive gift. Something sparkly, or meaningful, or luxurious. Instead Amy proposed, "I know how much your grandmother means to you and I would love to meet her. How about we take her out for coffee together, as your birthday celebration?"

I was speechless.

Amy was giving me the gift of her time. Her gift acknowledged my priorities. She found something priceless and gave me something you can't get in a store: validation.

Amy picked me up that afternoon and we drove to my grandparents' house together. When we walked through the door, she gifted them her homemade banana bread—because she remembered my saying it was one of their favorites.

We took my grandmother to a local coffee shop. We laughed and talked. My grandmother told her most prized stories and jokes. At every turn, Amy listened and found something in common with my grandmother.

Driving home from that visit, I was struck with a powerful thought.

Stop buying gifts. Start gifting time.

Giving a gift shows you are interested. Giving time shows you are invested. And there's a big difference.

Amy could have taken an interest by asking about my grandparents. Or looking at pictures of them. When she allocated her time, she invested in my family and in me.

I knew Amy was busy. Who isn't? A husband, two kids, plus a more-than-full-time job. That's why the gift of her time meant so much more.

If Amy could do that for me, could I do that for someone else? Could you?

I launched an experiment.

Two relatives, young girls, had upcoming birthdays. I made each one a gift certificate for a meal out at the restaurant of her choosing, in lieu of a store-bought gift.

At the end of the first gift night out, I asked for feedback.

"How was our dinner?" I inquired. "Were you disappointed you didn't get a gift?"

"I like this so much better than a gift!" she said. "Because this way we can spend time together!"

She was eight years old at the time. That's right. Even a child could tell the difference between interested and invested. Between a gift of money and a gift of time. And which gift was more valuable.

From that point forward, I viewed my calendar very differently. Because time was now a gift I could give. To myself. To my family. To my friends.

And so can you.

I started with gifts of dinners out. Then shopping trips. Road trips. Afternoon teas. Cooking meals to freeze with a friend who was having a baby. And even gifting myself workout time on my own calendar.

"That's a nice story," you might say. "But I don't have the time! You don't understand what it's like to be me!'"

Maybe I don't. So I'll ask you this.

> How often does your calendar dictate your priorities,
> rather than reflect them?

When you view your calendar and your time as a gift you give to yourself and to others, your calendar no longer runs you.

You run your calendar. You are in charge of the gifts you give.

You are finally freed from being a calendar slave.

What about the time equivalent of mindless spending, like watching TV, looking at your phone, playing online games?

In December 2015, *Time* reported, "The average person looks at his or her phone 46 times every day." And, *Digital Trends* quantified that those 46 phone views equate to 4.7 hours of time.

4.7 hours!

What would happen if you gifted just one hour of your social media or smartphone shenanigans to someone else?

How would your relationships change (the real ones, not the electronic ones)? How would you feel about the return on the investment of your time?

> When you change the way you value your time,
> you change the way you spend your time.

I experienced another shift when I changed my mindset about my calendar.

Even when I wasn't willing to pause my schedule for myself, I was at least willing to pause my schedule for someone else.

You might be the same way.

I couldn't handle the thought of a disappointed eight year old waiting for me at her favorite restaurant. So I kept an important commitment with my time.

"A ha!" you might say. "But I don't use a calendar! I prefer to be *spontaneous*!"

Perhaps that's why you're experiencing stress rather than success in your relationships and in your career.

Meet Joseph. Joseph is the life of the party. A great story teller, he's the friend everyone loves to invite to dinner. However, the smart hostess asks him to bring a dessert rather than an appetizer to share... because he hasn't arrived on time in decades.

Joseph is more than the good-hearted friend who forgets your birthday every single year. He's a man with a time management problem that almost cost him his best friend, his job, and his girlfriend. Because he never wanted a calendar.

One day he promised to get a rental truck and help me move. Fifteen minutes past our agreed meeting time, standing between mountains of cardboard boxes, I called him. I was greeted with a sleepy, far away voice.

"Are you still helping me move today?" I asked, barely masking my exasperation.

"Oh, friend, is that today?" he responded casually amidst a yawn and a stretch.

Joseph had an allergic reaction to the word "calendar" for most of his life. Why?

"It all seemed like way too much effort," he said. "I think the idea that a calendar equaled work started with my first Franklin Planner. The system was just way too complicated and time-consuming."

Arriving late to dinner eventually became the least of Joseph's concerns.

He'll never forget the conversation that startled him into time management reality, and that almost cost him his beloved job.

"During an annual performance review, my boss told me that I was doing a great job, my customers adored me and I was producing great results," he reflected. "But he told me I needed to get a calendar so that I could be a better manager and a better employee. That I could not go any further in my career without changing how I managed my time. It had really never occurred to me that my lack of a calendar affected anyone else. And could hold me back in my career."

Joseph made an effort to start using a calendar for work, because he understood the link between time management skills and *keeping his job*.

Outside of work, he failed to make the same connection, until the day his girlfriend almost called it quits because of his calendar.

"My girlfriend had rented a cabin in the woods for a weekend away," he shared. "Our first weekend getaway together...Except that I forgot to ask for the time off work."

Joseph lost time and money scrambling to make the trip. Worse, his girlfriend lost patience and it nearly cost him the relationship.

"I finally got a calendar," Joseph said.

Was the transition from pain to payoff immediate?

No. Joseph's intentions—to improve his time management skills—were good. Forming a new habit was challenging. And he found it easy to default to old patterns.

"I would still forget to put things on my calendar," he said. "Especially personal commitments. I almost missed a friend's wedding." Another wake-up call?

Joseph realized the reminders from his phone were much easier to deal with than the reminders from his angry friends.

What advice does Joseph have for converting from chaos to a calendar?

"Start small," he said, "and use reminders. Multiple reminders are your friend. Especially for important events. For example, for a friend's wedding, I might set a reminder seven days in advance. Then two days in advance. Then one day in advance. Then an hour before I need to leave. I just got tired of missing important stuff."

I asked him if family and friends had taken notice of his new calendar.

"They stopped complaining that I missed everything!" he exclaimed.

Joseph and I talked about the trade-off between time and money. And whether he's ever traded one for the other where his calendar is concerned.

"Yes, with my niece," he exclaimed. "My gift to her was, instead of buying her something for her birthday or for Christmas, to go out and eat ethnic food. Chinese. Japanese. Thai. She got exposed to foods she would never try. And we shared a lot of time together over the years by doing that."

If you're not using a calendar today, what gifts are you unable to give? And how often do you commit to a gift with the best of intentions, then fail to deliver?

Joseph's story is a great illustration of how to achieve *Success With Less* in your calendar. By taking one small step at a time. Acknowledging you will experience setbacks along the way in forming a new habit. And by prioritizing the most important people in your life.

Living a *Success With Less* life (a life with no regrets) means spending your time on the people and the experiences that matter most. As you consider how to give the gift of your time—to yourself, your family, your friends, and your colleagues—use the *Success With Less* formula to help guide you.

Pause to review how you currently spend your time and your money.
- Look at your calendar for the past month. What percentage of your time was gifted to:
  - You, for the gym, doctor, continuing education, sleep, vacation, alone time
  - Your spouse or significant other, for date night, meals at home, vacation
  - Your family, for childcare, events, time with extended family
  - Your friends, for meals, social events, visits
  - Your work, include commute time and after-hours emails and texts.
- Now look at your calendar for the next month. Whose birthdays will you celebrate? What gift-giving holidays are on the calendar? Which physical gifts could be replaced with gifts of your time?

Ponder the gaps between where you want to spend your time and where you currently spend your time.

- What is one way you would like to gift time to yourself that is not currently on your calendar (i.e., read a book, take an exercise class, practice an instrument)?
- What events or people do you want to have on your calendar that aren't there currently?
- Which meetings, events, and people add to your energy and enjoyment versus detracting from it?
- If you could start from scratch with the gift of your time, how would you allocate your time differently (you, family, friends, work)?

Prioritize how you spend your time and your money going forward.

- Remove calendar clutter.
  - At work, test your appointments against these key questions:
    - What is the purpose of this meeting?
    - Is this meeting with a person or about a topic that is important to me?
    - What would happen if I didn't attend this meeting?
    - Could someone else attend this meeting in my place?
    - Could this meeting be shorter in duration? Less frequent?
    - Could this topic be handled as effectively via email or voice mail?
  - Outside of work, test your commitments against these key questions:
    - Does my calendar include time to take care of myself (i.e., exercise, sleep, doctor's appointment)?
    - Do the events on my calendar involve the people who matter most (usually family and loved ones)?
    - Will failing to attend this event hurt or disappoint the people who matter most?
    - Is there a way to negotiate with family members to find another time to connect, so that you can attend this event?
  - Are you telling yourself a story about why you need to attend this event? And is the story true (e.g., "I'm the

only one who can be in charge of this event!" "My boss/spouse/friend expects me to be there!" "Everyone will be so disappointed if I miss this event!")?

- Reallocate TV time, mobile phone time, and social media time.
  o Designate one hour per week as a "no tech zone."
  o Choose one person to engage during that hour instead (that person could be you!).
- Choose two people to transition from your gift purchase list to your gift-of-time list.
  o Ask the person for feedback after you give the gift of your time.
- Finally, consider your new discoveries and your action plan—*and put those gifts on your calendar!*

6

Success With Less in Your Career

Every single day I'm on the receiving end of phone calls, emails, and social media messages like this: *Someone we both know said I should get in touch with you, because I'm looking for a new job. Could we (talk on the phone/meet at your office/have lunch) so I can introduce myself and tell you more?*

This entrée is often accompanied by the occasional side dish of a social media invitation to connect, follow or be followed. Some connectors serve up the full three-course-meal deal by proceeding to comment on one of my blogs or Tweets. #NotHelping

Guess what?

I'm not the only one on the receiving end of these requests. So is your boss. Your mentor. Your recruiter. Your hiring manager. That guy in HR.

And, by the way, you're not the only one contacting us.

The *Success With Less* Career Companion will help you prepare for a successful job interview, performance review or career conversation, so you can make the most out of these vital conversations.

Or, if you are self-employed, it could help you think about your strengths when presenting yourself to customers.

Conversations about your career are the conversations that matter. That's why I want to share the *Success With Less* Career Companion with you.

I have used this template with my team, my bosses and my coaches. Others have used the Career Companion to rotate jobs, find jobs, make connections, and get promoted. Download the one-page sheet, and let's take a look at it together.

You in a Few Words (Section 1)

What is the one question every single interviewer asks?

That's right.

"What are your strengths?"

Do you ever struggle to answer that question? I did. There's a balance between saying too little and saying too much.

When a question catches me by surprise, my answer always sounds generic, as I ramble on, trying in vain to make a point...

Then, I start thinking I totally blew it, which completely derails me when it's time to answer the next question.

Does that happen to you?

Here's what helped me. I noticed that when I would answer the strengths question, the interviewer would write down a couple of notes—usually in the margins on my resume.

One day I got curious. I glanced at the notes. Each interviewer was

Download your Career Companion at
successwithless.net/careercompanion

writing down three to five words that described me. Why?

When you interview multiple candidates for the same job, especially on the same day, it's easy to forget someone. At the end of the day, all the names blur together and it's hard to differentiate one person from the next.

The interviewer was writing down a few words to describe me—notes to help her remember me.

Jeff Bezos, CEO and Chairman of Amazon, says, "Your brand is what people say about you when you're not in the room."

I began to think of these "words in the margin" as my personal brand.

Consider this: If an interviewer is going to write down three to five words that uniquely describe you—words that will be said about you when you're not in the room—what words do you want the interviewer to remember?

When you answer the strengths question in run-on sentences, the interviewer chooses the three to five words.

What if you choose first?

Less Words = More Powerful

You now have the power to choose those three to five words.

How do you identify three to five impactful words that uniquely describe you and your strengths?

Apply the *Success With Less* formula to help.

Pause to research yourself.

- Brainstorm: Write down a list of all the words you would use to describe yourself. Remember, even if you are a karaoke champion, it's best to choose the words that apply to your career. Keep it realistic and positive. False modesty is still false. Go for the truth. You can handle it.
- Engage others: Ask your friends and family members to use three to five words to describe you. Write the words down. Then repeat the process with co-workers. If you prefer a more

formal approach, a simple, free survey to gather this feedback can be found at bit.ly/SWL_360Reach.

- Complete an online assessment: I like the *Clifton StrengthsFinder®* assessment because it generates a list of one- or two-word strengths in priority order. Each strength has an associated description. Take the StrengthsFinder assessment at bit.ly/SWL_Strengths.

Ponder to identify common themes.

- Look at the descriptions side by side.
- Circle words that appear on multiple lists.
- Consider what the repeating words and themes have in common. For example, do you see "always gets things done" on multiple lists? This indicates you are strong at *execution*. Do you see, "likes to figure things out?" This indicates you are strong at *complex problem-solving*.

Prioritize with three to five words you can easily remember.

- Which words best describe you?
- Which words reflect your marketable job skills?
- You can also choose the top 3 to 5 strengths from your StrengthsFinder assessment.
- Practice so that you are comfortable using these words to describe yourself in conversation.

Once you've identified your three to five words, list them in the "My Strengths" box of your *Success With Less* Career Companion.

You can use your new strengths statement:

- When meeting with a new boss or mentor for the first time
- In an interview
- In your follow-up email (as a reminder of your conversation and how your strengths are a fit for the role)
- As the headline on your resume and/or social media profiles
- As the opening statement in your bio or CV
- During a networking event

When you describe your strengths in three to five powerful words, you demonstrate that you have done your homework. You understand and can communicate what differentiates you from others.

Success With Less means you are now the author of your own short, powerful story. Using your words. To achieve your outcomes. On your terms.

You in a Few Examples (Section 2)

Once you've chosen the three to five words that best describe you and have practiced incorporating them into conversations, the next step is to build supporting examples.

Your strengths statement acts as an attention-grabbing headline about you. Your goal is to get your boss or your interviewer to want to hear the rest of your story.

Let's go back to the *Success With Less* formula.

Pause to choose your top two strengths.
- Focus on the one or two strengths that are the biggest enablers of your success. Consider a situation where you demonstrated your strength consistently.
- Review previous awards and performance reviews. Both provide clues about how other people observe your strengths in action.

Ponder two examples for each of your two strengths.
- In each example, include:
  - The situation when you started (i.e., total chaos, a recent budget cut or downsizing, lack of clear priorities, a start-up or launch, competitive threats, etc.)
  - What role you played in turning the situation around based on your specific strength. For example, hosted a team meeting to clarify priorities (*leadership*), managed a low-performing employee (*team-building*), or invented a new product feature to beat the competition (*innovator*).

     o   The measurable results you delivered (i.e., sales closed, costs or time saved, productivity improved, patent filed).

Prioritize the example your next audience cares about most.

- If you are meeting with your boss for your annual performance review, choose the example that helped *your boss* achieve a goal for the year.
- If you are meeting with an interviewer about a new job, choose the example that aligns with the new role you are seeking.
- If you're self-employed, pick what is likely to resonate with your customers (*leadership*).

- Practice delivering your success stories. Test them with a mentor or a co-worker. You can also record yourself and listen to the playback. The goal is to deliver your examples seamlessly, confidently, and conversationally.

Once you've identified two supporting examples, list them in the "Accomplishments" box of your *Success With Less* Career Companion.

You in a Few Career Next Steps (Section 3)

What do you want to be when you grow up?

I don't know either.

Which becomes a problem when a boss, a mentor or an interviewer asks the even-more-likely question...

> What job do you envision doing next at this company?

Do you ever struggle to describe your long-term career goals?

After years of fumbling with my long-term career goals answer, I finally came to a realization. I was putting an immense amount of pressure on myself to choose a specific job or a specific job title. That felt too narrow—too confining. It's the career equivalent of trying to find The One while dating.

I discovered it was much easier to describe *what I wanted to learn next*. I asked other people to help me match what I wanted to learn next with specific jobs and job titles.

Did it actually work?

Yes.

When I met with my boss for a career conversation, I opened with the strengths statement you developed in "You in a Few Words." Then, I used a supporting example like the ones you developed in "You in a Few Examples."

After that, I took the conversation one step further.

I used three to five words that described the type of role I was seeking next.

The conversation went like this, "I've enjoyed learning how to become an Innovative Sales Leader. Our sales have increased significantly over the last year. I'm wondering how else I could use my current skills while learning new skills. Strategy is an area that interests me, but I don't know where to get started. Who could you connect me with to help me learn more?"

Something interesting happened.

She connected me with the leader of Strategy and Planning.

You must be thinking, "Of course she did! That's so *obvious*!"

You're missing an important fact. It wasn't obvious to me.

I didn't know that such a department existed. I had never heard of it!

When I described what I was seeking, she knew exactly how to connect me.

And when you describe what you're seeking, your network of contacts will better be able to connect you, too.

Are you struggling to identify your next role? Let's use the use the *Success With Less* formula to help you describe what you want to learn next.

Pause to do your research.

- Brainstorm: Write down a list of all the skills you would like to build. Add any experiences you would like to have (i.e., travel globally, present to executives, etc.). Add any exposure you would like to gain (i.e., a different department, a different style of boss, the opportunity to spend time with customers).
- Engage others: Seek out people who currently have those skills—friends, co-workers, former bosses. Ask what their jobs are like on a day-to-day basis. Ask what it takes to be successful in their jobs. Ask how long it took them to become an expert at a particular skill. Be *actively* curious.
- Go online: Which skills are in the most demand? Which jobs have the greatest number of postings? What classes, professional certificates, and networking groups are available in your areas of interest? Read job descriptions as well. Job descriptions provide clues about what you might want to learn next—clues about how your skills might be an asset in those types of roles.

Ponder to identify common themes.

- Look at your list of the education, experience, and exposure you are seeking to gain. Compare that list with feedback from your conversations with others and online research.
- Circle themes that appear on multiple lists.
- Consider what the repeating themes have in common. For example, do you see skills involving systems and processes? This indicates you may be looking for a role in operations. Do you see spend time outside of the company? This indicates you may be looking for a role in sales or public relations.

Prioritize with three to five words you can easily remember.

- Which words best describe what you want to learn next?
- Which words reflect your marketable job skills?

- Ask others for feedback. Go back to the people you talked with in the "pause" phase. Ask them if your description sounds like a reasonable next step from your current role. This is also great practice to get comfortable sharing the description of what you want to learn next. Practice first, before conversations with your boss, a recruiter or a hiring manager.

When you describe what you want to learn next in three to five words, you make it easy for your network of contacts, your boss, your recruiter and your hiring manager to help you. You also come across as having a well thought out plan, and a sense of purpose.

You will quickly and easily identify who is in a position to help you achieve your goals...and who is not.

As you look for your next role, you must continue to perform at a high level in your current role. This is even more critical if you are looking for your next role within the same company.

Once you've identified three to five words that describe what you want to learn next, list them in the "Next Role" box of your *Success With Less Career Companion*.

You in a Few Career "Must-haves" (Section 4)

Now that you have evaluated your current strengths and your accomplishments, let's consider where you want to go next.

I'll never forget a friend who called me during a lull in my career to interview me for a job that was "just perfect" for me. I charged ahead into the interview process for a role that I have never once coveted in my entire career.

Why?

Without a clear destination in mind, I was prone to detours.

When I'm approached with a new opportunity, it's incredibly flattering. My talents are "finally" being recognized! And, after all, haven't things been frustrating lately? Maybe the grass really is greener somewhere else…

Have you ever had the "grass is greener" thought?

You might even go as far as I did in the interview process, getting to a written offer. You may consult a friend, a spouse or a mentor for advice. You may review the details of the compensation package, the job description, and the title.

Ultimately, though, how do you know if this job is right for you?

Understanding your priorities in advance will help you make decisions based on facts rather than flattery.

Success With Less means being laser-focused on a short list of your career "must haves" versus "nice to haves" before a job opportunity is eminent.

Thinking about your must-haves in advance will help you avoid career regrets.

Ponder to identify what matters most.

- There's a difference between nice-to-haves (free gummy bears in the break room) and must-haves (not willing to relocate) in your career climb.
- Reflect back on jobs you enjoyed where you succeeded. Then reflect on jobs you enjoyed. Maybe you were at your job, but it drained your energy. For example, I had a boss who would hold a team meeting every single day to get an update on our sales forecast. I was miserable. Being micro-managed made me feel like I was not trusted or empowered. That was an important clue for me. A career must-have for me is a manager who trusts and empowers me to do my job.

Prioritize your three to five must-haves.

- The must-haves that rise to the top for me time and again involve geography (whether or not I'm willing to move, how much/how often I'm willing to travel).

- For me, the characteristics of my manager are key. I know I need someone who identifies and maximizes my strengths, and has *transferrable intelligence*, which means that they are expert at something and are able to teach me what they know.
- Review your own priorities before circumstances change in your career. Your must-haves are your guide to what you really need. You will also avoid the buyer's remorse of taking a job that's not right for you or that does not align with your life goals.

Remember that job opportunity I described earlier, where I was referred by a friend? I was flattered, but I discovered it wasn't the role I wanted. I didn't want to hurt my friend's feelings by not pursuing the job, though.

If I had established my career "must-haves" in advance, I never would have applied for the job, much less gotten all the way to an offer.

Why?

Because the job was 100% commission. And one of my must-haves is a base salary. The job required having a network of relationships and I had no contacts to get started. One of my other must-haves is being able to use past skills and contacts in new ways. This job met none of my most important requirements.

I could continue, but my point is this: I could have saved the time and embarrassment of turning down the job with two simple sentences.

Thanks for thinking of me for this role. I know it's not a fit for me based on my pay requirements and the skills the job requires up front.

Boom.

It's that simple.

And who is going to argue with your personal priorities?

I'll give you a hint: no one.

No one is going to say, "You should really take the job that will put you on the road 52 weeks a year, now that you've just had twins."

No one is going to say, "You should definitely relocate even though your mother is dying, and you're her primary care provider."

The simple response to your priorities?

> Thanks for letting me know. I'll keep you in mind
> if something that's a better fit for you comes along.

Knowing what you want makes the conversation easy for you, and easy for the other person. In the end, you have the same goal: a great fit.

You in a Few Lifetime Jobs (Section 5)

The Chief Customer Officer of a Fortune 50 company shared the ups and downs of her career path with me over dinner one evening.

"Stop envisioning the perfect job," she told me. "Start envisioning a lifetime of jobs."

Her bold statement opened up a world of possibilities to me in a time of corporate restructuring, re-organization, and pervasive budget cuts. Perhaps my entire career path was not narrowing down to one single point—the "perfect job"—rather opening up to a career of careers.

According to the Bureau of Labor Statistics, the average worker currently holds ten different jobs before age 40, and this number is projected to grow. Forrester Research predicts that today's youngest workers will hold twelve to fifteen different jobs in their lifetime.

What does that mean to you?

It means you could find many "perfect" jobs based on your variety of interests and talents throughout the course of your career.

You and I have focused on assessing where you are right now.

Now let's think big. Let's consider your Career of Careers. Every role that could be of interest to you in the future.

All that matters in this part of the thought process is what interests you.

Pause to consider these questions.
- If you could write your own job description within your current company, what would it be?
- If you started your own business, what would it be?
- Are you interested in consulting or teaching?
- When you were in junior high, what did you want to be when you grew up?
- When other people remark, "You would be great at _____," what fills in the blank?
- When you meet people and learn about their jobs, what makes you say, "I could *totally* do that! That sounds like fun!"

Ponder to identify common themes.
- Look at your list of jobs and ideas.
- Circle the themes or jobs that are similar or easy to connect.
- Compare these jobs and themes with your career must-haves. What words, phrases and ideas repeat themselves?

Prioritize your career of careers short list.
- Choose three core themes that show up repeatedly on your list. For example, when I look at my career must-haves next to my career of careers list, I identify three consistent themes: flexibility, variety and autonomy. What does that mean to me?
    o Flexibility: I am at my best when work is a thing I do, rather than a place I go. I do not want to physically report to the same office every day at the same time. I want the flexibility to choose whether I conduct my work at home, at the local coffee shop, or out on the road.
    o Variety: I am at my best when I am solving complex problems. Once the solution is identified, I'm not at my best implementing steps 1-999 of the solution. I need the variety of new problems to solve and new challenges to address to stay engaged and motivated.

> o Autonomy: I'm at my best when I know what's expected of me and the problem that needs to be solved. Then I need the breathing room to go solve it.

- What are your three themes? Identify the common experiences of how and where you would spend your time based on your list. These are great reflections of your priorities and your preferences.

Right now you might be thinking, "But I'm never going to have all these jobs! Why bother?"

I'll show you. It's time to put the pieces of the puzzle together.

First, list your career of careers, business ownership interests and ideas.

Cancel your power lunch. Feast on your *Success With Less* Career Companion instead.

It's time for you to take center stage in your career conversations.

Consider each conversation script as a starting point. You will need to make adjustments to fit your style, your audience and your situation.

How to ask for a meeting:
*I'm a (insert your strengths statement from **You in a Few Words**) seeking a (insert your 3-5 word career statement from **You in a Few Career Goals**). (Insert name of contact) referred me to you because you lead a team in my area of interest and are currently hiring. What's the best way to schedule time for us to meet?*

You will instantly know whether or not your contact is in a position to help you, because you've clearly stated the kind of role you are seeking and the strengths you would bring to the role.

How to answer questions in an interview:
Question: What are your strengths?
Answer: Use your description from *You in a Few Words*.

Question: Give me an example of a time when you used your strengths to deliver results in a previous role.

Answer: Use your description from *You in a Few Examples.*

Question: What other jobs could you envision doing next at this company?

Answer: Use your description from *You in a Few Career Next Steps.* You could also respond with common themes from *You in a Few Lifetime Jobs.*

How to have a career conversation with your boss or mentor:

> *Currently, I think my strengths are (insert your strengths statement from **You in a Few Words**). A few examples of how I've turned my strengths into results are (insert your statements from **You in a Few Examples**). Do you agree? (Pause to let the other person respond.) I've been thinking about my career in terms of what I want to learn next. And I'm interested in (insert your 3-5 word career statement from **You in a Few Career Goals**). What roles do we have at our company where I could use my strengths and also learn something new?*

You will demonstrate the ability to do your own thinking, instead of asking someone else to do your career planning for you. You will immediately engage your boss to identify gaps between how you see yourself and how your boss sees you. Finally, you will engage your boss or mentor in helping you find your next role.

Now that we've applied the *Success With Less* formula to your career, let's move on to your relationships.

7

Success With Less in Your Relationships

Your toxic relationships are keeping you stuck at a crossroads.

Imagine this. Your phone is ringing right now. You glance down to see who's calling. What's your immediate reaction?

Groan and hit decline—or answer enthusiastically on the first ring?

Your first reaction when you see the caller's name is a toxic thermometer that instantly registers an undeniable reading.

The same gut test holds true for your calendar. When you see who's on your calendar for the next week, how do you feel?

Frequently, relationships in my life register a toxic reading. And yet that poison still appears repeatedly on my calendar. In prime time spots. Eager to consume the best of my energy.

It doesn't have to be like that.

Success With Less in Your Relationships is about applying what you already know about your calendar and about your career. Then taking those lessons learned one step further—one more step towards a life with no regrets.

When it comes to relationships:

Success With More = Breadth

Success With Less = Depth

When you fill your life with acquaintances, you achieve relationship breadth. When you focus on a few important relationships, you can achieve relationship depth.

When I am stuck at a crossroads, experiencing a setback or a loss, I want relationships with depth in my life.

But we only have so much time and energy to build and sustain relationships with depth.

Relationships with depth are reserved for people whose calls you enthusiastically answer on the first ring. Maybe it's because they've stood at your crossroads with you, supporting you and helping you move forward.

I'm talking about the Refrigerator Rights people.

That phrase refers to the people in your life who come to your house, open your refrigerator, and get their own food or drinks—without asking you and without you feeling weird about it.

I'm paraphrasing a concept that Dr. Will Miller introduced in his thought-provoking book, *Refrigerator Rights*.

Does the thought of someone opening your refrigerator without your permission make you feel uncomfortable?

Me too.

To open someone else's refrigerator without permission requires a relationship of some depth, right? A high degree of comfort is required. You are vulnerable, but there's no fear. You're not worried about how the other person might react to amazing leftovers that are now a moldy science fair project. Or that the only secret about your family's famous salad dressing recipe is that it comes straight from a grocery store bottle.

Refrigerator Rights relationships mean you're willing to share your imperfections. Because how often does the inside of your refrigerator look perfect?

Now take the Refrigerator Rights concept one step further. How many people in your life have Refrigerator Rights access to your heart? Who gets to open the vacuum-sealed door to your feelings without asking permission? Who gets to see the emotional science fair project lurking in your deep, dark corners?

In short: who gets to see the real you?

My Refrigerator Rights list is very short by that definition. I'm willing to bet yours is, too. Yet those are the relationships I value the most. And the relationships that we need the most, when facing a crossroads.

The challenge is: how do we transition from a life filled with casual connections to a life filled with Refrigerator Rights relationships?

By taking time to clean out the refrigerator.

Just like your kitchen refrigerator has a limited amount of space, so does your relationship refrigerator. Just like some of your groceries have a limited shelf life, so do some of your relationships. And it's time to start exploring which relationships were meant to have a limited shelf life. And which ones have long since expired.

Before you start rehearsing your, "It's not you, it's me speech," take a deep breath.

Because the first relationship you and I are going to get serious about is the relationship you have with yourself. The way you see yourself. And the way you see yourself in relationship to other people.

When my refrigerator is full, the labels obscure the light.

That's a problem. Because when I'm trying to take stock of what's in my refrigerator, and whether or not it's still worthwhile, I gravitate toward the labels. And then assign a relative value to the contents to decide what I'm going to keep and what I'm going to discard.

What does that have to do with anything?

When I can't see the light on the labels, I'm prone to misinterpretation. To filling in the blanks with my imagination. Making it much more difficult to assess the value of what's behind the labels accurately.

Do you know where I'm going with this?

In *"Success With Less* in Your Calendar" and *"Success With Less* in Your Career," you envisioned an ideal version of "you." The version where you gift the time on your calendar differently. The version where your career goals align with your life goals. And you achieve your goals. The version where you shine bright in life.

But something is standing in the way of illuminating that version of yourself. Otherwise, you probably wouldn't be reading this book.

What's blocking your bright light from shining every single day? What's obscuring your vision of yourself?

All. Those. Labels.

You are secretly afraid that someone is going to open your emotional refrigerator, read all of the labels on your proverbial shelves, and then judge your worth as a person.

Here's a life-changing secret.

It's your refrigerator.

And the only labels on the shelves are the ones you choose to put there.

You have the power to clean out the labels that no longer fit. You can put them in the trash and let them be carried away permanently.

Labels only have power when you put them in prime viewing spots. Then shine a bright light on them. And stare at them. Repeatedly.

How often in everyday conversations do you use labels like these to describe yourself—or someone else—accompanied with a value judgment?

Single. Married. Divorced. Widowed. Gay.

Downsized. Right-sized. Demoted. Unemployed.

Fat. Thin. Short. Tall. Bald.

Whatever it is.

The way you view yourself, the way others view you, will only change when you describe yourself as you wish to be seen, without judgment.

When the story I tell myself is, "I didn't get enough done today," "Nobody cares about me," "I am not enough," I proceed to tell a version of that same story to other people as well.

When the story I tell myself is, "I accomplished so much today," "I have so many people in my life who care about me," "I am enough," I proceed to tell a version of that same story to other people as well.

So, I shine my brightest light on the second set of labels. The labels I choose. Because getting rid of old labels leaves space for my bright light to shine through. You can, too.

You've already taken a baby step toward changing the labels you put on yourself.

What would happen if you replaced your emotionally charged labels with a description of what you're good at instead?

How would your confidence change? How would your conversations change? How would you see yourself differently? How would others see you differently?

When I describe myself differently, I see myself differently. And in a much better light. That conversational shift in how I describe myself to others creates a mindset shift.

When I repeat what I do well using labels I choose, I feel confident. Empowered. Focused. Understood. And those same feelings are possible for you, too.

Cleaning out the old labels you've used to define yourself is the first step toward achieving *Success With Less* in your relationships. And a helpful confidence builder to attack the second part of your assignment.

Now it's time to evaluate the expiration date on your relationships with other people.

"Pleeeeeeeaaaaaaaaaaase, don't make me!"

I felt that way, too. Until I thought back on a couple of my toxic relationship experiences, where I hung on way too long. To my own detriment.

Have you ever dated someone, known you needed to break up, and then kept right on dating the same person? I have. Or worked for a toxic, maniac of a boss who is running you into the ground and then worked even longer hours at the same job? I have. Why is that?

I know why I did it. First, I let my old labels limit my future options. That's why I had to change the labels I used to describe myself. And so do you.

But there's something else. I hung on to expired relationships too long because I became paralyzed when I pictured the break-up discussion.

So, instead of breaking up, I decided to stay together. And you have made the same choice. The choice to live in your own misery, rather than make someone else miserable. No matter how miserably that person is treating you.

That makes no sense!

But you and I do hold on to our misery all the time.

Just like eating expired food will make you miserable and sick, feasting on toxic relationships will poison your chances to live the life you dream.

The common denominator in this equation is you.

Which leaves two choices. Continue to live in misery, falling short of your goal of a no-regrets life. Or make those necessary endings. Clean out your relationship refrigerator.

What's standing between you and your next level of success is a few. More. Endings.

> Getting to the next level always requires ending something, leaving it behind, and moving on. Growth itself demands that we move on. Without the ability to end things, people stay stuck, never becoming who they are meant to be, never accomplishing all that their talents and abilities should afford them...[1]

Wait—give up?

Yes. Sometimes to exit your crossroads. Sometimes to go to the next level. You have to give up. You have to quit. You have to leave some relationships behind.

"But quitters never win!" you're saying to yourself. Repeating an age old adage. And a damaging label.

Dead. Wrong.

Quitters win all the time. Quitters who win learn to quit the right things. Winners quit at the right time.

Because quitters who win in life know this: The good cannot begin until the bad ends.

Endings are difficult. Endings are emotional. Endings take courage. So, why bother?

---

[1] Dr. Henry Cloud, author of *Necessary Endings: The Employees, Businesses, and Relationships That All of Us Have to Give Up In.*

What if I chose to stay with the same doctor who had misdiagnosed me? What if I stayed in the same draining dating relationship? Or with the same toxic boss? Where would I be right now? Probably not writing this book.

Probably even more ill. Even more miserable. Even more exhausted. Even more down on myself.

Probably right where you are at this very moment. Stuck. Frustrated. And still dreading the break-ups you know need to happen.

Here's the key: I didn't end those relationships all at once.

I didn't find a new doctor the same day I broke up with my significant other and quit my job.

I started with one toxic relationship—the one that was causing me immense and immediate pain. I started there.

"But if I end relationships, people will think I'm a failure!" you're screaming on the inside right now.

I've felt that way, too. What I learned is that there's a canyon-sized gap between failing and failing well.

Dr. Cloud describes the difference in an empowering way.

> Failing well means ending something that is not working
> and choosing to do something else better.

Choice.

There's that word again. That one word that gives you and me the power to make a change.

My choices were: Stay with the same doctor and be sick or find another doctor and get well. Stay with the same partner who was disrespecting me or reclaim that energy for myself to invest in other ways. Stay with the toxic boss who was dragging me down or find a new job.

You are afforded the very same kinds of choices in your situation.

"If you are looking for the formula that can get you motivated and fearless, here it is: You must finally see reality for what it is—in other words, what is not working is not going to magically begin working. If something isn't working, you must admit that what you are doing to get it to work is hopeless," writes Dr. Cloud.

When I confronted the reality in my toxic relationships—that they were not going to change—it was easier to choose another way. I chose a better way. And you can, too.

When I make the choice to end a hopeless relationship, I am confronted with a range of emotions. And you will be, too. Relief. Fear. Grief. Anxiousness. Hope.

Not all at once. Not just once. Not always in that order.

Here's what is waiting for you on the other side of that emotional roller coaster, after failing well:

A life of no regrets.

I do not regret choosing a new doctor and getting well. I do not regret ending a draining relationship and showering myself with affection instead. I do not regret leaving my toxic boss behind and finding a work environment where I can thrive. Not for one second. And you won't either.

Still resisting your necessary endings? Leaning against the door to your relationship refrigerator so you don't have to look inside?

Here's one more thought from Dr. Cloud:

If you feel resistance about executing a certain ending, figure out what two or more desires are in conflict, admit to yourself you can only have one, and then ask yourself this question: Which one am I willing to give up to have the other one?

Right now. Today. Who do you choose? Yourself? Or some spoiled relationship leftovers in your refrigerator? Which one are you willing to give up to have the other one?

Use the *Success With Less* formula to guide your thought process.

Pause to take stock of what's in your relationship refrigerator.

- Labels

  o Review the strengths statement you drafted for your *Success With Less* Career Companion. How do you feel about yourself when you review your strengths?

  o Imagine you're introducing yourself to someone at a party for the first time. What labels do you use to describe yourself consistently? How do you feel when you use those labels in conversation?

- Relationships

  o Imagine your phone is ringing. It's time for you to consider your own personal, internal caller ID. Who should you ignore? Whose calls do you want to pick up on the first ring?

  o Look at your calendar for the next week. Who do you dread seeing? Who do you look forward to seeing? Who should be on your calendar, but isn't?

Ponder which labels and relationships are expiring or expired.

- Labels

  o Which words would you add or change to better reflect your strengths in your career conversations?

  o Which words would you add or change to better reflect how you represent yourself in everyday conversations?

- Relationships

  o Who are the two most toxic people at work with whom you spend the most time?

- o Who are the two most toxic people outside of work with whom you spend the most time?

- o Who are the two people with whom you would like to spend more time?

Prioritize where to start cleaning out your refrigerator.

- Labels

  - o Use your strengths to describe yourself at work.

  - o Use your revised description of yourself in all conversations.

- Relationships

  - o Choose one work relationship to end and set your target timeline. (Note: If that relationship is with your boss, use your *Success With Less* Career Companion to start seeking a new job or to start a new business.)

  - o Choose one personal relationship to end and set your target timeline.

  - o Choose one person to add to your calendar, as you are phasing out the two relationships above.

Changing relationships—especially ending them—takes time and courage. Choose one at a time.

You won't achieve *Success With Less* in Your Health until you address the toxic relationships in your life. And your health is the next stop on your journey toward your *Success With Less* life.

8

Success With Less in Your Health

Your brain is your biggest ally in the battle of the bulge.

Because your muffin top has more to do with your mind than with your muffins.

How is that possible?

Your body functions like a highly efficient version of the invest versus divest trade-off.

And when your brain is trying to deal with more—more calendar commitments, more toxic relationships, more stress—then your brain ravenously prowls for more energy and for more nutrients.

The only way for your brain to gain more energy and more nutrients is to give less energy and less nutrients to the rest of your body.

Have you ever noticed how much more likely you are to get sick when you're under extreme stress? That's your body's invest versus divest principle at play.

When you stuff your brain, you starve your body. When you stuff your body, you starve your brain.

Is it possible to simultaneously nourish your body and your mind? The answer might surprise you.

The answer is "yes," by pressing pause, to give your body and your brain the vacation they both desperately need.

After getting treatment for pesticide poisoning, my body was not the same. Although the numbers on my test results inched me closer toward Health Valedictorian, I was only focused on one number: the number on the scale.

Except that number wasn't changing.

No matter how many hours I spent at the gym. No matter how many diet plans I tried.

Have you ever been there?

I was so upset, I authored a new set of fairy tales to mask how I was really feeling.

"I'm just so thankful I was correctly diagnosed. I feel so much better, and that's what matters most!"

Which was true. I was grateful to feel better and to be better. But I also wanted to look better. And, my guess is, so do you. My Doctor suggested fasting, which may or may not be right for you.

What pressing pause on food consumption periodically taught me is the value of pressing pause on the other excesses I constantly reached for in my life. Out of habit.

Activity. Approval. Accomplishments. Acceptance.

Just like you.

I could not achieve *Success With Less* in my health until I achieved *Success With Less* in my calendar. And in my relationships. I could not have a healthy body until I had a healthy mind. I could not reach for healthy habits until I cleaned out what I stocked on the shelves in my refrigerator. And the same is true for you.

It took a change in my food habits to understand what I needed to nourish myself.

"If you remove the things that are toxic to you—emotions, chemicals, foods, people—whatever that toxic exposure is," Dr. Logan explained, "and instead you add the nutrients that are going to nourish the body—positive emotions, whole foods, exercise, healthy relationships— you give your body what it needs to be well.

"Your body has 75 trillion cells that work every single day to create balance. All of those cells intrinsically know how to achieve balance," Dr. Logan continued. "Your choices are what's preventing your body from getting what it needs to make and to keep you well. Your mind can't outsmart your body."

The good news is that you are not alone in your fight to achieve optimal health.

You have the power to put 75 trillion resources to work for you every single day. By sending out the command signal with the choices you make. What you eat. Where you spend your time. With whom you spend your time.

If your body is willing to battle for you, why aren't you willing to battle for your body?

According to my doctor, as humans, we don't like to be deprived. We don't like to be told we can't have or do or be something.

You and I fight the desire for more when our bodies are designed for less. Less food. Less stress. Less chaos.

Food is the first battle you will fight to claim victory in *Success With Less* in your health. But food fights are not the only conflict brewing on your horizon.

Because the sum total of your health results from more than the number on your scale.

After I worked fasting into my schedule consistently, Dr. Logan proceeded to kill my long-held beliefs about exercise.

I managed my exercise routine like I managed the rest of my life: in a dead sprint from one activity to the next. In a race to the finish line.

I was literally always on the run.

Are you trying to keep pace in that same race?

"Running is not good for you," Dr. Logan plainly stated.

What?

How are you and I going to stay ahead if we get off the treadmill?

"People love to hear this," he chuckled. "Basically when runners get into the zone and achieve the runner's high, they have very little heart rate variability. For heart health, you need wide variations in heart rate and blood pressure. Instead of running long distances, you need to do interval training."

Your body is designed to be pushed to the limit. And then to take a pause. To refresh before the next period of peak performance.

Which means you don't need more hours of exercise. You need more recovery periods between short bursts of intense exercise.

You were designed to run in a relay race. Not in a marathon.

In a relay race, you run while someone else rests. Then you rest while someone else runs. The key to victory is ensuring a seamless transition from the person in motion to the person at rest. Which takes practice.

And I was years out of practice at how to transition from being in motion to being at rest. My guess is, you are too.

I learned to treat my body like we were in a relay race together—on the same team—competing for a shared prize. Coordinating a series of stops and starts changes the race.

But I realized I needed one more fierce competitor to join my winning team.

My mind.

Transforming my body ultimately proved easier than transforming my mind.

Your mind is the ultimate racer. Always running ahead of you. Introducing hurdles and asking you to jump to conclusions as you sidestep from worry to worry.

I was no exception. When I went to bed at night, my mind was still reeling from the day's activities. Making a mental checklist of tasks undone, worrying ahead to task lists two days from now...and criticizing myself for tasks left undone.

I had learned to create pauses in my calendar. My food intake. And my exercise routine.

But I struggled to create pauses in my mind.

(You're worried I'm going to invite you to yoga now, aren't you?)

I'm not.

While yoga is an effective way for some people to quiet their minds, yoga did not work for me. I was too overwhelmed when I envisioned an entire hour dedicated to quieting my mind.

So I had to start smaller. And you might need to do the same.

Two approaches enabled me to quiet my mind long enough to hear my own voice.

1. Journals.

2. Sunsets.

When I started a journal, I started small. No requirements for length. Frequency. Or topics. My goal was to create a place for the voices in my head to take center stage. At a matinee hour instead of a midnight showing. So that I could literally rest easier.

My other rule? I didn't reread what I wrote. So I wasn't tempted to look in the rear view mirror. And to revisit decisions I could no longer change.

Keeping a journal was a game changer. Because I released my deepest thoughts. Without judgment. And, I was challenged to engage in other activities while writing in my journal.

In fact, I enjoyed the benefits of keeping a journal so much that I slowly added one more brain break. Watching the sunset.

Sunsets are my way of exhaling. Of enjoying the moment unfolding in breathtaking wonder in front of me. Without the slightest feeling that there's somewhere else I would rather be. Or something else I would rather be doing. I noticed I enjoyed watching the sunset on vacation. So I wondered, *Would I experience the same soothing effects watching the sunset at home?*

I sat on my back patio one evening. And watched the sun slowly dip behind the clouds. Painting the sky in a vibrant array of colors. For ten glorious minutes.

I felt so relaxed and at peace I wasn't even tempted to look at my phone.

One feeling emanated from the inside out the moment the sun flattened to a red-tinged pancake across the horizon. Gratitude. I was thankful for the sunset. For the breath I was taking. For that very moment. Peace. Serenity. Calm. Presence.

I started looking forward to the next sunset. Because I felt more refreshed after watching the sunset at home than I had in entire hours of formal meditation classes.

The key was finding what worked for me. What felt effortless and enjoyable. Almost irresistible. And the same is true for you.

How much time does it take for your brain to refresh?

Just like you don't need to run for hours to train your body, you don't need to meditate for hours to train your mind. Ten minutes a day, or three minutes three times a day, to pause and relax can be sufficient.

What happens when your body and mind work together to run the relay race of your life?

You finally achieve *Success With Less* in your health. One step at a time.

I'm living proof.

I'll never forget the appointment I had with Dr. Logan eight and half years into our journey together.

"How are you feeling?" he asked.

After years of searching for clues in the tone of his voice, I proceeded cautiously.

"I don't know," I responded slowly. "You have my test results in that folder on your desk. Why don't you tell me how I'm feeling?"

Silently expecting the worst.

He paused. Then opened the yellowing manila folder on his desk. The folder that had held the contents of my hopes and my dreams. My despair and my denial. Countless times through the years.

"You are the picture of health," he exhaled. "We finally did it!"

But I still held my breath.

After almost nine years. Countless setbacks. Radical reinvention. I could hardly process what he was saying. As a highlights reel of years of ups and downs sitting in that very same office played in slow motion in my mind.

And when I allowed myself to breathe again—to be fully present in that moment—to process what he was sharing...

I.

Instantly.

Felt.

Lighter.

Not just because I weighed less than before my health crisis started (although I did). But because I finally understood how it felt to be weightless.

I finally unloaded the heavy baggage that was weighing me down for most of my life. I lightened the load I was carrying. By slowly removing labels that no longer fit. Toxic relationships. Activity addiction. Regrets. And a formula for success that no longer measured what mattered to me.

In that moment, I was free of seeking Success With More. And free to live *Success With Less*.

You, too, can be weightless. You, too, can travel with a lighter load. Achieving *Success With Less* in Your Health is about more than cutting calories, and reaching your ideal size and weight. Being healthy means managing your calendar. Your career. Your relationships. Your stress level. And revisiting how you measure success.

Use the *Success With Less* formula to help.

Pause to take a health inventory.

- Diet
    - Go slow to go fast. Reduce your calories. See what happens if you reduce your calorie intake. Did you survive? Go out and treat yourself to a beautiful sunset or other calorie-free reward.
    - Pause to remind yourself: You. Can. Do. It.

- Exercise
    - o If you want to create a change (wait for it...) maybe you need to create a change! Mix it up in the workout department. Here's one small change that can make a big difference: Reduce your cardio workout time by half. Then change your workout to include two minutes of running with one minute of walking in between. Or two minutes of jumping rope or biking and then one minute of walking.
    - o Change your routine for one week and then take a pause. How are you feeling now?
    - o Just make sure you move every day!
- Recharge
    - o Watch the sunset and leave your phone in the car.
    - o Phone a friend you haven't spoken with in more than a month.
    - o Garden, or walk through a garden.
    - o Read a book or a magazine.
    - o Watch a video or listen to music that inspires you.
    - o Sing or play your favorite instrument.

Ponder the fact that the gap between your current health and your ideal health is smaller than you think.

- You know what to do. You know how to do it. What's missing? Time. Take the time to take yourself towards the new you. That journey happens with one step, one day at a time. All you have is this moment, right now. What's more important: that bagel or your health?

Prioritize the first health gift you will give yourself.

- Choose one area to get started: food, exercise or recharge/relax.

- Engage resources around you for support: books, apps, online support communities, physical trainers, friends and family.

You matter more than any food that has ever been created, cooked or served. Your health is the most delicious dish you will ever savor.

It took me years to realize that my love affair with food was a relationship with the wrong priority. Your health is your gift to yourself, to your loved ones, to the people around you.

When you make food more important than yourself, you give in to a lie—a fairy tale that doesn't have a happy ending. Do you know what the lie is?

You've heard that "you are what you eat." But what happens if you are *more important* than what you eat? Food isn't the priority. Your health is.

Invest or divest. The choice is yours. And the right choice is easier than you think, when you make yourself the priority.

Please remember that the Hippie Doctor is not your doctor. And, my body is not your body. So, before you try this or any other nutrition or exercise plan, consult your physician.

9

Surviving a Setback—What to Do When You Default to Old Habits

Experiencing a setback is the best opportunity you have to reassess your values. And your priorities. To decide whether or not what you value is still worth pursuing with the best of your energy.

Even though that evaluation process is painful. And sometimes time consuming. I know. I've been there.

Here's what I learned: When you're running in the race of your life, setbacks are inevitable.

No matter how great your intentions. No matter the intensity of your effort. Your clarity of purpose. Who you know. How much money you have. Or the extent of your training.

I remember the first time I took an unplanned detour.

It was a physical detour that became an emotional journey. Filled with the same emotions you might be experiencing right now while trying to live *Success With Less* in your calendar. Your career. Your relationships. And your health.

After training for months to compete in a half marathon, race day finally arrived. I followed the training plan exactly as outlined. I bought new running shoes. Socks designed to ward off blisters. I carb-loaded. (Dreamy!) I hydrated. And there I was on a beautiful Saturday morning standing at the start line. Watching the sun rise over the city skyline.

Moments before the race began, I did one final safety check. I made sure my house key was still fastened securely to the inside of my running shorts.

The starting gun sounded and we were literally off to the races. Shoes pounding the pavement in blissful unison. Finding our pace. Hitting our stride. Everything was going according to plan.

Four miles into the race, I felt the sudden urge to check on my house key. Weird, right? But I wanted to make sure what I valued most was still secure. You know where I'm going with this, don't you?

It was gone.

Do you know that feeling when you can't find your car keys and you're running late for an appointment?

It was like that feeling. Except I was literally running. In a marathon.

My body surged forward while my mind raced backward. My key *must* be here somewhere! Temporary disbelief. Just keep running! Activity is always the solution.

What if my key is not here? Panic.

Don't drop out of the race now! Hold on to hope.

How could my key not be here? Anger.

I tore myself apart mentally while my body physically defaulted to old habits. To learned patterns. Keep putting one foot in front of the other. Use constant activity as a way to run from my problems.

How often do you default to old habits when you're facing a setback? How often does the story in your head prompt you to distance yourself from the reality of your situation? How often do you try to just keep running?

Eventually the competing voices in my head overpowered the sound of my shoes on the pavement. Imagining my worst-case scenario left me paralyzed, unable to compete effectively in the race for which I had trained.

I trotted over to the side of the road. My body pulsing with adrenaline. My mind racing. I checked my pockets. My waistband. My sports bra. The ground around me. I even checked my ponytail. (Desperation is a strange thing.) My house key was definitely gone!

Now what?

A crossroads moment.

Childhood training prevailed when I saw a police officer nearby. "Yes," I recalled. "When in trouble, ask a police officer for help." It was the most rational thought I had had in several minutes.

I approached Officer Burly whose heaping muscles only served to make him seem larger than life in my situation. I was like a child relaying a holiday wish list to Santa. Filled with the belief that he would magically grant my one wish of finding my house key and successfully finishing the race.

My words poured out in a slur of adrenaline and panic.

"Need help. Key gone. House key. Feel sick. What do I dooooooooo?"

"The only thing you can do," he said, matter of fact, "is to run the race in reverse and look for it. There's nothing else we can really do to help you other than call lost and found."

What?

You're the expert who's supposed to help me. And the best advice you have is... go backwards?

When someone speaks the truth in your situation, especially during your setback, how do you respond?

I had the same responses you do. Assign blame (to someone else). "If that cop was better at his job, there would be more options."

Enter denial. "Impossible! There must be other options to consider. This is not hopeless!"

Give in to fear. "Someone probably already found my key. And is breaking into my house right now! Robbing me blind! While I am out here sweating in the hot sun!"

Hang on a minute. That last part makes no sense!

That's what you're thinking right now. There is no possible way someone found your house key and your house, given that you did not lose your driver's license with your key.

And that's the power of fear. When fear takes over during your setback, as it might be right now, it is paralyzing. You imagine the worst. Even though the worst has already happened. You tell yourself a story that isn't true. Because your imagination feeds on fiction, not facts. And then you repeat the story to yourself over and over until you are convinced you will not survive your setback. You sabotage yourself.

That sabotage is the gateway to becoming deeply disillusioned. It's about that time when you start to see your circumstances relative to everyone else around you. Through the lens of your deeply disillusioned state.

I stood motionless with fear. Imagining a devastating home robbery. I saw the same runners filtered through a new, more distorted perspective. Everyone was moving forward so easily. But I was stuck. Everyone looked carefree. But I was in crisis. And I couldn't help but feel jealous of their progress. Their seeming lack of obstacles. We used to be on the same path, but we were no longer competing in the same race.

Have you ever felt like that in life? Are you feeling that way right now?Like you're standing still while everyone else is passing you by. Like everyone has it easier than you. Like no one else seems to experience setbacks. Like everyone else has a clear picture of their goals and always makes forward progress. Like you've been sidelined in the race of life. Relegated to the disabled list.

I've felt that way, too.

Here's the issue. I made the choice to stand still. While everyone else kept moving.

I made the choice to measure my progress relative to everyone else around me.

What if, in your setback right now, the only person choosing to stand still is you?

That's harsh, isn't it?

I'm speaking the truth in your situation. Just like the police officer spoke the truth in my situation.

I know that doesn't make it any easier to hear.

When you make the choice to stand still, you drain the very time and energy you could be using to live a life with no regrets. And you will continue to see the problems on the horizon in your situation from the same point of view while you are standing still. Just like I did.

When I was forced to choose between divergent priorities—run backwards to find my key or run forward towards the finish line—I was forced to focus my energy and my attention on the single goal I cared about the most. I was relieved of the pressure to "do it all." Because, in my situation, "doing it all" was literally impossible.

Just like you can't do it all in your life either. You can't fit all those appointments on your calendar. You can't transform your diet and your career and your relationship with your partner and your kids all at the same time. You relieve yourself of the pressure to do it all the moment you simplify. The moment you choose the one goal that matters to you the most right now.

111

Crossing the finish line in a life of no regrets means taking a series of small, incremental steps. One at a time. Together.

When I was forced to simplify and to reset my own expectations of success, the mile-marker signs on the side of the road held up by someone else, no longer mattered. Why?

Because the mile markers no longer accurately measured my progress. Because the mile markers no longer accurately reflected how far I had traveled. Because the mile markers no longer accurately represented how I defined success. Or how much farther I needed to progress to realize my single, simplified goal.

In life, you and I are tempted to focus on the signs and measure of success held up by the crowd standing on the sidelines, watching you run your race. Look in the crowd, do you see your parents? Your siblings? Your bosses? Your best friends? Or that mysterious pack of judgmental observers in life you and I refer to as "they" and "them."

As in, "What are *they* going to think if I quit now?" "Will they still want me to hang out with *them* if I don't have an important job title?"

> Never look back unless you are planning to go that way.
> - Henry David Thoreau

It's time to transfer the power of measuring *Success With Less* from *them* to *you*.

Because *they* don't wake up in your life every day. *You* do. So, why do *they* get a vote?

Here's something else I noticed. When I was running toward the finish line, it seemed like I hadn't progressed far enough fast enough. Suddenly everything changed. When I looked back toward the start line, I was reminded of how far I had already come. A perspective I completely lost while I was in constant forward motion.

It's like the feeling you have at the end of every day. When you scold yourself for all the tasks you didn't accomplish, instead of congratulating

112

yourself for all the tasks you did accomplish. You have already made substantial progress on your journey. Celebrate that.

But progress is always relative to perspective.

Which is why two miles into my reverse road race, my perspective changed. Again. Actually, my perspective was literally overshadowed by a looming figure in my peripheral vision.

A bus.

Why a bus?

You're thinking, now she gets hit by a bus? No, I promise. I don't get hit by a bus. And you won't either.

In any road race, there's a minimum allowable pace per minute. And a bus follows along at that exact pace to pick up the stragglers. Yes, I was about to get picked up by the slow bus.

And here's an interesting lesson about progress and perspective when you're experiencing a setback. I looked at that bus as representative of failing—failing on two fronts. Failure to reclaim something valuable I lost—my key. And failure to achieve my goal—finish the race.

What would happen if I viewed that bus instead as helping me to arrive, at just the right time?

Same bus. Same driver. Two different points of view.

The bus driver opened the door. "Would you like a ride?" he asked with a smile. "We'll take you as far as you need to go."

There I was in the throes of a desperate situation. The help I needed arrived just on time. The help was available at no additional cost. Offered by an expert. All I had to do was take the first step. And, I refused the help.

Why?

Because I was determined to prove I could reach the finish line on my own. Even if that choice meant regressing further. And draining the rest of my fading energy.

Are you saying "no" to help and "yes" to your setback?

Someone—me, your boss, your mentor, your spouse—is offering you the help you need. And you refuse to take it. Probably for the same reason I did. Because the helper was telling me something I didn't want to hear: I couldn't achieve my goal. My way. On my ideal timeline.

So, instead of accepting the help, I kept going. Just like you. Draining even more energy. Just to prove I could do it myself.

Interestingly enough, help continued to follow me. Just like help—in the form of the concepts in this very book—continues to follow you.

The bus kept pace with my slow pace. In fact, help followed me for several miles.

Even though help was persistent, I was resistant.

Are you ever like that?

It almost always takes a breakdown to reach a breakthrough, as you and I have discussed.

My breakdown that day? I finally lost so much momentum, I had to get on the bus. I literally couldn't take one more step on my own. Because I was too exhausted to continue my search.

That's right. I failed to achieve my goal.

What would change for you, right now, if you said yes to help—and you quit waiting until you have no other choice?

The moment I quit and got on the bus I overheard the driver tell another passenger, "Don't you worry," he laughed. "We drive this bus right across the finish line of the race."

When I crossed the finish line that day, I was handed the same medal as everyone else. The same band played. The same crowd cheered. Even though the way each runner reached the finish line was completely different. Even though we arrived there at a different pace. Even though some of us had help along the way.

You and I are in this *Success With Less* journey together. I'm just like you. I've faced multiple setbacks. I've lived through the loss of people and jobs and beliefs about myself that I valued. I've figured out how to survive these setbacks, and you can, too.

The key is to run your own race. At your own pace. To start small. To keep moving. To establish your own measures of success. To accept help when it's offered. And to accept the medals—those little rewards along the way—for valiantly surviving your setbacks. To reward and congratulate yourself for having the courage to lead a *Success With Less* life.

10

Living the *Success With Less* Way

Success With Less is more than a formula. And more than my story. There are other people already living the *Success With Less* way. Dreaming big. Surviving setbacks. Reprioritizing. Simplifying. Trying again. And succeeding.

Like my long-time friend, Katrina. You always experience Katrina before you actually see her, because her infectious laughter and her kind spirit echo throughout every aspect of her life. And yours. As she effortlessly draws you into her warm, genuine vibrancy. She is the friend you trust with your deepest, darkest fears, who loves you through your setbacks even while she's navigating countless crossroads and setbacks of her own.

Katrina's life story reads like a sensational tabloid. With so many unexpected twists and turns you tell yourself, "I'm so glad something like that could *never* happen to me!"

Until one day the same unthinkable setbacks happen to you. Health crisis. Divorce. Financial ruin. Katrina has faced all those setbacks, and more, in her quest to live a life of no regrets.

Katrina's story is about how to overcome the seemingly impossible. How to rise again after you fall. How to live beyond your labels. How to overcome countless odds that cause others to count you out.

And if you count Katrina's success merely by the numbers, you will be tempted to dismiss her for the powerful role model that she is.

Thirteen years. Eight cities. Two children. Six career changes. One life-threatening illness.

Katrina dreamed of a happy, healthy family. And a career in healthcare. While trying to juggle the demands of medical school, marriage, and mothering toddlers, Katrina lived in a state of constant chaos.

Just like you and me, Katrina not only wanted to have it all, she also wanted to have it all right now. And to have it all right now, she tried to do more. So she could have more. So that she could be more.

Do you ever get stuck in that endless loop?

Katrina was paying the cost of being more at the expense of enjoying less.

"We finally purchased a house right when I was starting medical school," she reminisced. "And I thought, *finally*, my dreams are all coming true! Well, we were scheduled to move the same day as the white coat ceremony [a ritual that marks the beginning of the program] at my school. None of my family or friends attended the ceremony because they were busy moving our boxes."

She didn't know if this was the new beginning she needed—or just the most depressing way to face her new life.

She paused long enough to notice a yield sign. She wondered if she should continue down the same path or turn back. But the demands of homework and getting settled in a new home launched her back in motion. Prematurely.

Katrina continued forward at breakneck pace. Sacrificing sleep. Exercise. Nutrition. She was exhausted constantly. Barely functioning on a daily basis.

And ignoring all the signs she was headed toward a disaster. Until she absolutely crashed.

"I flunked a class. I had never flunked a class in my entire life! It was a serious wake-up call. I was giving up time with my family to fail on every other front! I wasn't just failing a class, I felt like I was failing in the class of life," she recalled.

Her yield sign from months before started to look more like a stop sign.

"The instructors called a meeting with me to discuss how to make up the work," she said. "I called my husband to ask what I should do—make up the class or drop out. I was so exhausted at that point. And, for the first time ever, he said to do what I wanted to do. So, I called the doctors and told them I was quitting the program."

Katrina recalls that as the first time she ever paused long enough to listen to her own voice. And then to make her own choice.

She felt relieved after making the decision to resign from medical school. And to focus on finding a career that enabled her to enjoy her family and her life.

Just because she gave up on her classes, though, doesn't mean she gave up on her dream. Instead, a career in healthcare became her dream deferred.

Katrina realized she couldn't be a doctor. And a wife. And a mother. *right now*. If she could only have one *right now*, she decided to choose her family. Because she didn't want to miss precious time with her children.

Katrina had no regrets about choosing her family. Especially when she encountered the setback that changed her life forever:

Stage III breast cancer.

Her significant setback was devastating on every level. She was in a fight for her life, literally. She tried to survive by doing what she had always done: more.

"Funny you talk about how you couldn't do more. At one point, I was scared my husband was going to leave. Because, at that point, I called someone I trust who is an expert at doing more. She gave me tips on how to do more. I knew she was crazy. I knew I couldn't do more. *I had cancer!* There was no more to give."

Then, another "big reveal." Mid-treatment, her husband announced that he wanted a divorce.

Her suspicions confirmed, Katrina spiraled into despair. She went from doing more to doing less to doing nothing.

"I could barely get off the couch," she shared.

How did she find the energy to rise again?

"Help came in the form of other people," she said. "When you get cancer, people want to be helpful, so they mail you gifts. I got lots of pink clothing, pink ribbons, pink everything. And the gifts were great. But what got me off the couch was getting a routine again. Friends inviting me to do fun things. I'm a social person. And because of that, I would make myself get off the couch occasionally to go to lunch with someone."

Gifts of time mean more than gifts of stuff to someone who is facing a setback. And you are in a position to give life changing gifts (just like we discussed in *Success With Less* in Your Calendar).

And Katrina attributes her redemption story to being on the receiving end of countless gifts of time.

The gifts of time went beyond lunch dates, to preparing meals for the family, and more. Driving her kids to after school activities. And even hosting Katrina and her kids for mini-vacations when her health started to improve.

Surviving a health setback gave Katrina another gift. The realization that the time to live her dreams was right now. Because she knew she literally had no guarantee of tomorrow. And she still wanted to live a life of no regrets.

So she returned to school after a decade-long pause. She earned her nursing degree—providing a way for her to spend time with her children and to enjoy the career of her dreams.

What's it like to realize a dream deferred? I wondered.

"I think people might think living your dreams is this overpowering wonderful, amazing, emotional thing. That's not it. It's a journey to that feeling. It's more like slowly realizing I'm finally comfortable. I'm finally back where I'm supposed to be. I'm not lost in the woods anymore. It doesn't mean I won't walk back into the woods. But I feel peaceful. For the first time. In a very long time. In a very, very long time."

You, too, might feel like you're wandering in the woods. Looking for the light in your dark situation. Katrina's story is a great reminder that you, too, can overcome anything. Even the loss of one of the most important relationships in your life. When Katrina lost her spouse, she gained a new level of support from family friends. She was not alone, and neither are you. Even in the midst of significant setbacks, you, too, can realize your dream deferred.

What if realizing your dream deferred involves taking a significant risk?

How do you decide whether to go all in or to take the safe route?

Meet Erica. Erica had a big decision to make—to trust her gut and go all in on the biggest risk of her career...or to play it safe and take the easy path.

At work, Erica was a rising star. The teammate everyone wanted. The boss everyone sought out. She had endless options and many promotions still ahead. The voices around her—her team, her peers, her boss—told her to just keep going.

But there was one problem.

Erica's internal voice was quietly telling her a different story. The time had come for her to pursue her bold, new idea. It was time for her to make a change. She realized that the path for everyone else was not the path for her.

For her career to progress further, Erica would be expected to take on more. More employees. More projects. More responsibilities. But, everything inside her screamed one word, "Less!"

Erica wrestled with her decision for months, until the voices inside of her became louder than the voices around her. And she knew she would live to regret playing it safe.

Finally, Erica transferred all of her employees to other managers. She reversed her highly coveted career trajectory *in a day*. Everyone thought she was crazy.

Well, not everyone. She had a few friends. And she would need both her resolute belief in her idea, and the few friends that believed in her, to survive the setbacks that were still ahead.

And then, Erica took her beliefs, her friends, her ideas...and turned her "crazy" idea into 2.5 million followers.

"I knew the only way I could succeed at this crazy idea I had was to focus on building one single success story. I couldn't think about all the future challenges. Or focus on the risk. I had to focus on what I could deliver right now. Because I was taking a huge gamble to build out a new concept. And I knew I only had one chance."

What was Erica's idea?

Erica envisioned creating a way for her company's customers to easily connect with each other. Customers often told her they wanted to talk with other companies who were facing similar challenges. Implementing the products and solutions for the first time. Instead of working through the tangled web of support cases and training employees about how to use the products, these customers wanted a way to easily learn from each other.

Erica knew she could introduce her customers to each other. But she realized that idea would only scale to reach a limited audience. So, she imagined something bigger. Something bolder. An online platform to automate the process of connecting customers to each other. And then, she wanted to connect her company's employees with those customers. She wanted to take action, based on the customer's concerns and on the customer's ideas.

She burned the candle at both ends—simultaneously burning favors with her limited circle of sponsors—to create her first success story. Just when she expected to be elevated for her efforts, she was depressed nearly to her breaking point.

"We had a huge event for our executives and our customers," she recalled. "During the question and answer session, one of the customers stood up to thank the company for creating this new program. And then asked how the company was going to invest in the program going forward."

The executives on stage, supposedly the largest supporters of her new program, looked at one another. They exchanged blank stares, as they wondered who was going to respond.

Erica held her breath. It was a simple question! She was waiting for someone—anyone—to explain how important it was to move forward and describe (even in simple terms) the company's commitment.

As she listened intently to the silence, then the backpedaling, then the complete lack of support or understanding from her "leadership team," she flashed back on the late nights, the lost weekends, the vast amount of emails...Was it all for nothing?

The silence was deafening. Until she was thunderstruck with a realization. She was standing alone.

Her executives had no real knowledge of the program she toiled to build. And they didn't understand today's value well enough to envision tomorrow's investment in her program. Or in her.

She watched as the illusion of her career breakthrough melted like an ice cream cone on a hot summer day. What she thought was progress was just a huge, melted puddle of confusion. And she witnessed the meltdown right before her very own eyes.

But Erica wasn't done. Not yet. She still had some bold moves left to make.

"I was scared to death. It's one thing to feel like you've got a huge team of people behind you...but when there's no one—not even your own executives watching your back—that's so scary!" she exclaimed.

In a last-ditch effort to salvage her career, Erica took the bold step of tweeting the entire team of unsupportive executives, during the awkward question-and-answer pause.

She felt she owed it to herself—and to her customer—to set the record straight.

Are you thinking, "Oh no! Don't hit send!"

She hit send.

Erica had reached the breaking point. While anxiously awaiting a response, she texted her husband. "I might be losing my job."

The next ten minutes felt like ten years.

Ping! A reply tweet had arrived.

Much to her surprise, the response contained a public apology. To Erica and to her customer.

Moments later, she received a private message with a request from the executives.

A request to simplify her story. To make the value of the program easier to understand.

To remember.

To repeat.

Her executives were literally asking her to deliver more, with less.

So she went back to the drawing board. To edit the story she was telling about herself. About her customers. And about her program. To remove old labels that no longer served her purpose. Just like you did in *Success With Less* in Your Relationships.

Her initial description was:

> *The customer online community is a way for customers to connect with each other while showcasing our company's technology, because the solution is built using our own products. Customers help each other solve problems. And also submit ideas. We then turn their ideas into the next products on our roadmap. And also create raving fans in the process… and on, and on, and on.*

She simplified to a single, high impact sentence:

> *The online community is a single hub for our customers to get their questions answered, to share their ideas, and to network with each other and with us.*

Her new approach worked! Her executives could now see through the clutter to embrace her bold claims.

Do you ever feel like you're not being heard? That's the value of completing your *Success With Less* Career Companion. To make your story and your intentions heard. Just like Erica encapsulated the value of her program in one sentence, you can encapsulate your value in one conversation.

Ultimately, Erica created more engaged executives by saying less. When she simplified her story, she multiplied her results. And you can, too.

Ten years later, the program Erica created has 2.5 million followers. And that's not all.

The vote that was stacked against her became a unanimous vote in her favor.

"Normally conversations about who is going to get promoted—especially for higher level promotions—involve hours upon hours of conversation and contention about each candidate," she explained. "When our company President opened the discussion about my promotion, the discussion lasted less than five minutes."

Which was as long as it took for the President of the company to ask, "Why have we waited so long to promote Erica? What is wrong with us?"

When Erica received news of her promotion to Vice President, she knew she had earned more than a raise and a new business card.

"I've never had a promotion mean more to me personally and professionally, because it validated that my decision to take a chance was the right one," she said. "But my promotion also meant something to the entire community of customers I had been championing. They were waiting for the validation that they mattered, too. And so my promotion also elevated them."

Erica advanced herself, her customers, and her entire industry. By listening to her heart. Trusting her gut. Believing in her dreams. Drawing strength from the friends who believed in her dreams. And pausing to listen to her own voice.

11

The Payoff for Living *Success With Less*

Closing the gap between where you are now and living *Success With Less* is a step-by-step journey.

Some steps will feel light and effortless, while some steps will feel heavy and treacherous. There will be moments when you hope someone else will carry you. I had the same experience.

Why continue on this journey then? Why keep putting one foot in front of the other?

Because there's a payoff awaiting you. A reward worth pursuing. If you keep going.

A life with no regrets.

Do you want to live a life with no regrets?

I know I do.

Together you and I have explored a few key steps you can choose to take. With your Calendar. Your Career. Your Relationships. Your Health.

Like you, I'm tempted to skip steps. Misstep. And sometimes even over-step.

And I'll never forget the time I actually counted my steps.

When I applied the *Success With Less* formula more consistently to my calendar, I achieved a major breakthrough. There was actually white space on my calendar. Competing, colorful commitment blocks were replaced with whimsical white space. Freedom. Breathing room. Perhaps for the first time in my life.

Instead of being overjoyed, I was anxious at first. Uncomfortable. I had to fight my natural urge to fill my newfound white space with meaningless activities. Old habits die hard. Can you relate?

Instead, I paused. When I paused, I pondered what I would enjoy doing with that time. Then, I prioritized the people and the experiences that mattered most. It wasn't easy. Which is why I shared my ideas with a few friends. Because I knew that would create the accountability I needed to follow through on my intentions.

Pause + Ponder + Prioritize = Success With Less

When I paused to simplify my life, what I cared about rose to the top of the list. Because there was finally room in my mind and in my calendar for that to happen. It was like cleaning out an overstuffed closet. Or that junk drawer that won't open. Because it's jammed full of crumpled, food-stained carry out menus, expired coupons, dilapidated matchbooks, and pencils with broken tips. The junk that's consuming the limited space you have to store your valuables.

When you clean out the excess junk in your drawers, you're left with a clear, unobstructed view of what you value the most.

When you clean out the excess junk in your life,
you're left with room for someday dreams to become today's plans.

How?

You've heard of the domino effect: one action that sets off a chain reaction.

Well, I felt like I had been pushing single dominos for years. Trying to find the one that would set off the positive chain reaction. The payoff for the pain. Maybe you feel that way, too.

What's on your "someday" list?

What would happen if you chose three somedays and started planning them today?

When I started planning my three somedays, I went from hopeless to hopeful. Because my dreams would no longer be deferred. I realized my dreams were within reach, and that fact alone energized me.

I went from scattered to focused. Simplifying to a short list of three goals enabled me to spend my limited time and money with a sense of purpose. I refused to let meaningless meetings and frivolous spending detour me. And I established clear boundaries to safeguard the space reserved for my dreams.

I also realized this: someday is right now.

How many regrets would I carry with me if I failed to live those someday experiences?

Do you want to live a lifetime of too late?

I don't.

The first hint of having made the right decision came disguised as a postcard in the mail. The author list for the library guild luncheon. I could hardly believe my eyes.

One of my most admired authors, Gail Sheehy, was going to be there. In person! In my town! What would I wear?

I've kept Gail's book, *Passages*, in my bedside table since I was 18 years old. I have read her insights about the passage I am living every month since then. Her book is my North Star.

The library luncheon was now more than a way to spend time with my aunt. The library luncheon was now the place where I would meet my hero.

In fact, I took my copy of *Passages* with me to the authors' luncheon. Along with a little courage. And a copy of Gail Sheehy's newly released autobiography, *Daring: My Passages*.

When I approached Gail at her table, the entire room around me appeared animated. The lights looked brighter. The colors looked more vibrant. The voices sounded louder. My entire experience was amplified.

My heart started pounding. My breath was shallow and rapid. All I could think was, "Is. This. Really. Happening...to meeeeee?"

Yes. It was.

How would that experience have changed, if I flew in (just under the wire) to sit down for lunch? Then kissed my aunt on the cheek, before bolting at the first break to take a conference call. (I had done exactly that many times before.)

But not today. Not this time. This time was different.

I wasn't going to miss this experience.

Are you missing out on important experiences? And people? And moments... In your own life?

It doesn't have to be that way.

Because there's another way.

You have the power to choose your experiences. You have the power to say yes. You have the power to say no. And, you, yes, you, have the power to be present to enjoy the experiences you choose.

Well, the line to meet Gail felt like it stretched on to eternity...even though there were only two people in line ahead of me. Instead of diverting to my phone to mindlessly pass the time, I peered around the people in front of me, to sneak peeks at Gail. I was amazed that a woman who was so big in my mind was so tiny in person. A huge life force was compressed into petite packaging.

The two dawdlers in front of me ambled away in most leisurely fashion. I tried to refrain from literally jumping up and down. Luckily I succeeded—there was no jumping.

Just as the last of the polka dot dress on the lady in front of me faded from view, there she was!

And there *I was*. Present in that moment. Nothing obstructing my view. And no more obstacles standing between me and my goal.

I stepped toward Gail. A pen was perched gently on the tips of her fingers, much the way it might have been when she first started her writing career.

Well, I never could have predicted what happened next.

Gail invited me to sit down. "I'm thrilled to see that old, worn out copy of *Passages*," she said. "Writing that book was a breakthrough moment for me."

As she inscribed and autographed both books, I told her about my story. How I had come to know her work. And how it had become a part of my life.

Remarkably, our story didn't end there. After reading her autobiography, I submitted my personal story online to her "Daring" website.

Two days later, an email in my inbox caused me to blink once. Twice. Three times.

Hello Karen,

Thanks for sending in your Daring story, which I like very much. It's a great example of listening to your inner voice in your Trying Twenties, accepting a "failure" (a called off engagement), as

My fingertips lit up the keyboard like a summertime bonfire! Hot on the trail of another memory-making moment.

Gail had interviewed Margaret Thatcher and Hillary Clinton. Would she remember me from the library luncheon encounter?

Every ounce of anxiety melted away the second I heard her voice. Still warm and welcoming; now familiar. The two-hour conversation elapsed with the ease of an afternoon dialog with a lifelong friend.

I reveled in every single second. Not wanting our conversation to come to an end. I had waited my whole adult life for this moment!

As our conversation came to a close, I asked her for some advice.

"You've been interviewing people for years. And studying patterns tied to aging," I said. "I have a milestone birthday coming up this year. Do you have any advice?"

"Take another couple of trips," Gail said. "Think about scaling the parts of your life you haven't paid attention to—maybe explore your artistic side or your community involvement side. This is the time of opportunity."

> This is the time of opportunity.
> What are you going to do with it?

I'll tell you what I did. I quickly proceeded to make plans for item number three on my short list—climb the Sydney Harbor Bridge in Australia.

Here's what I didn't realize at the time. That bridge would become a physical manifestation of my personal journey, putting actions to my feelings. A script to my experiences. And symbolizing, for me, *exactly* what it means to rise above your challenges.

Your baggage.

Your past.

I inhaled sharply when the object of my dreams came into clear view from the airplane window.

I confidently proclaimed to my fellow passengers, "I'm going to climb that bridge this week!"

After seeing that very same bridge—that very same goal—from the ground, I was tempted to retract my bold proclamation.

Because, from the ground, the Sydney Harbor Bridge is *really* tall.

Insurmountably tall.

In fact, there were people actually climbing the bridge at that very moment. They looked like tiny ants on the distant horizon. Suspended over...what is that? Oh, yes, *very deep water—and a highway*!

Beads of perspiration instantly formed across my face.

> When you gaze at your goals from the ground,
> do they look lofty and unattainable?
>
> But how far will you be able to climb,
> with your feet firmly planted on the ground?

I stood motionless and transfixed. Looking up at the towering bridge. If I stayed in my safe zone, I would miss my bridge appointment.

When I imagined how I would feel describing a failed bridge climb attempt to others, one word immediately came to mind: Regrets.

So, I took just a few, small steps forward. And so can you.

In my case, the steps took me to base camp, aka the training ground for my climb.

As I walked toward the building, I noticed a huge banner that read, "The Climb of Your Life."

And that's when it struck me: You and I are on the climb of our lives. Literally. Right now. Each and every day.

It starts with a few...more...steps.

If only you and I are willing to take them.

Inside base camp, I learned there would be an expert guide on my journey. Special equipment. Training. And the opportunity to practice in a safe environment before making the official climb.

I was still nervous.

What if I physically couldn't endure the climb? What if I somehow fell off the bridge?

Here's the reality: I had already fallen off the bridge. When I ignored my health. When I crowded my calendar. When I prioritized doing over being.

All the fears that haunted me had already happened. And I had survived.

So have you. You are already a survivor. You are already successful. You are already capable. You just need to be reminded from time to time.

And so did I.

When our guide led us across the iron platform toward the bridge, I looked out across the group assembling for the next training session.

I paused to look up to the top of the bridge. Sunlight twinkling off the highest beam.

At that moment, there were 1,332 steps between me and success.

When I fixed my gaze on the goal—the top of the bridge—I couldn't see the individual steps. When I started the journey toward my goal, though, I immediately lost perspective. I looked down and focused on every single step. How quickly I could climb the steps. And how many steps were left to climb.

This is the beauty of taking an expert with you on your journey. An experienced guide will help you focus on what matters most. To prioritize what you need to bring with you to succeed on your climb. To elevate your focus from where you are right now to where you have the potential to go. To see the setbacks that lie ahead, and to prepare you to overcome them.

And ultimately to get out of your way so you can enjoy the view of what you've achieved.

I am offering to be your guide on the climb of *your* life. Just like an experienced climber helped me take 1,332 steps from base camp to my personal goal, I am here to help you climb. To rise to the level of success you dream of in your own life. One step at a time. And to make sure you don't miss the breathtaking view of your own life along the way.

I'll never forget the wise counsel the guide shared during the bridge climb.

"You are on the climb of your life right now. How often are you going to climb this high? If we rush straight to the top, you'll miss the view. This isn't about getting to the top as quickly as possible. It's about being conscious of every single step. And how our point of view changes as we rise. Unless I remind you to take a pause, you'll miss all the moments that matter along the way."

Do you pause long enough to enjoy the moments that matter along the way in your life?

How does your point of view change when you rise?

The further you rise, the better the view. The further you rise, the more worthwhile the effort. The further you rise, the more rewarding the journey.

It took an expert. Many experts, in fact. To teach me to pause and to enjoy the view along the way. To remind me to enjoy the climb of my life. To help me slow down on the climb to the top.

And now I'm here to do the same for you. To help you focus your energy and your effort to make it to the top in your life. And to enjoy the view along the way.

How did it feel to reach the top of the bridge?

Deeply fulfilling. Almost overwhelming. The wind was blowing gently through my hair. The sun was just beginning to set through parted clouds. And I had a clear view of the famous Sydney Opera House.

But I had an even more interesting view in the opposite direction.

It was a view of my company's local office building. After all the struggles with my calendar and with my career, I had finally risen above my work—both literally and figuratively.

It was amazing how small work looked when I saw it from an elevated point of view, against a vast and varied landscape of possibilities.

I had triumphed ever so briefly over fear. Doubt. Activity addiction. And I was finally enjoying the view.

Are you enjoying the scenic view of your own life?

Or are you so focused on executing every single step that
you're missing the breathtaking landscape surrounding you?

When you focus on the day-to-day, you miss the bigger picture. Of who you are. Of what you can achieve. Of what you're already achieved.

Success With Less is a tool to bring into focus what matters most to you. The delta from where you are, to who you really are, starts with three steps: Pause. Ponder. Prioritize.

You don't have to travel around the world to experience the climb of *your* life. You can start right now. At home.

Use the *Success With Less* formula to make a short list of your priorities. Share it with a friend or family member. And then...

Just. Keep. Climbing.

12

Join the *Success With Less* Journey

Success With Less is *your* story. *Your* journey. The climb of *your* life.

What I learned is that I needed others to join me on my journey. Empathizers. Experts. Encouragers. I couldn't succeed alone. And you can't either.

That's why I'm inviting you to share your story. To connect with me and with others who are learning to live *Success With Less*. Choice by choice. Day by day. Month by month. Year by year.

Maybe you're just getting started. That's okay. Maybe you've already survived a setback and are facing a crossroads again. That's okay, too.

I've been there. And so have many others. It's easy to let fear rule our lives. To convince ourselves we've gone as far as we can go. Or that living a life without regrets is beyond our reach.

When I'm feeling that way, I like to read one of my favorite passages from Marianne Williamson's book, *A Return To Love: Reflections on the Principles of A Course in Miracles*.

> *Our deepest fear is not that we are inadequate. Our deepest fear is that we are powerful beyond measure. It is our light, not our darkness that most frightens us. We ask ourselves, Who am I to be brilliant, gorgeous, talented, fabulous? Actually, who are you not to be? ... Your playing small does not serve the world. There is nothing enlightened about shrinking so that other people won't feel insecure around you. We are all meant to shine, as children*

do... And as we let our own light shine, we unconsciously give other people permission to do the same. As we are liberated from our own fear, our presence automatically liberates others.

You, too, are powerful beyond measure.

It's your turn to shine. It's your turn to be liberated. It's your turn to inspire others.

Acknowledgements

Success With Less is more than a formula. It's the story of my life's journey. And I would like to thank some of the many people who have made that journey better and more enjoyable.

First to my Hippie Doctor turned friend, Dr. Kevin Logan. You are a diligent, patient, kind caregiver. From you, I've learned a new way to be well—mind, body and spirit. Thank you for restoring my health, the greatest gift of all.

Bill, Jim, and Diane. You are my career-refresh trifecta. I had no idea that transforming my career would ultimately involve transforming my life. You invested deeply and consistently. And you encouraged me to own and to share my story. Thank you.

Kirsten. I only said yes to giving a motivational speech for your conference because of how much I respect you. Secretly, I was dreading it! Thank you for providing a platform to tell my story. Your reaction and the audience reaction is what encouraged me to write this book.

Dr. Joe. Thank you for living my life's passages with me. You continue to teach me something new with every email, every call, every conversation. You have the gift of tireless, caring repetition, even when I'm a slow and stubborn learner.

Ann, Katie Jo and Regan. Though we're miles apart, you're always close to my heart. Thank you for your emails, calls, texts, and visits. You are my cheerleaders when I lose hope and my friends no matter what! Thank you for seeing me at my lowest and loving me anyway.

BDJ. There is no algorithm on the planet that pairs us as lifelong friends. And that's what makes our decades-long adventure exciting, unpredictable, and most memorable. Thank you for always doing maintenance and never letting on when it gets old. You smell nice.

Book Club Girls. Even if you never read this book, I hope you at least read this sentence. Thank you for listening, loving, laughing, and luxuriating with me for over 15 years. You have never wavered in your support through so many ups and downs. Let's grow old together!

Rodney. You are my only friend who serves drinks (when needed) in the driveway. Thank you for helping me laugh at myself. Let's be honest, there's a lot of material! And thank you for not publishing my damaging, tell all book before I did. LOL!

John and Michael. You always feed my stomach. More importantly, you feed my soul. Thank you for making me part of your extended family. For late night sing-alongs around the piano. And for being willing to read early drafts of this book!

Tanya. You are my dream weaver and champion. Thank you for our date nights. Our accidental nine-mile walks with taco breaks. And for sustaining my power of belief. The belief that anything is possible, even writing a book! I wouldn't want to share a silverware BFF necklace with anyone else!

HRH. You have shown me the world, literally and figuratively. Your ability to deliver the royal treatment is beyond words and beyond measure. Thank you for bursting into song with me in person and via text. Because of you, there's within my heart a melody.

Beau and Johnny. To my brothers from another mother, you make holidays and every day in between better. Thank you for being an extended part of my family and my steadfast supporters. We have too many fun memories together to count at this point! Here's to many more.

TV and Amy. You are living kindness. From our early days of working together and every day since, you've taken an active interest in my health, my family, my friends, my career, and my life. Thank you for sustaining our friendship across years and companies. I'm thankful to know both of you.

Mama D and Nancy. Two words: Baking Days. We laugh, we cry, we rage, we feast, we bake. And the cycle begins again. From Christmas in July to Barefoot recipes, you two are a treat!

Marilyn. Thank you for always listening. Always caring. For multiplying my joys, and dividing my sorrows. For tearing up with me when there are no more words. Sixteen years and counting! (Can you believe it?)

My family, The Englands, The Wandlings and The Woodalls. Thankfully, there are so many of you who've been kindness and joy, it's impossible to name you individually. From card nights. To girls' weekends. To Sunday dinners. To holidays. To family vacations. To dance recitals. To leisurely breakfasts. Sporting events. And so much more. Thank you for your love and support.

Joseph, Katrina and Erica. Thank you for allowing me to share your stories. Your journey toward a *Success With Less* life is an inspiration.

Thanks also to Kristen Engelhardt, and to my extended family at Salesforce, for helping me to dream big.

Finally, to Chris Westfall. You made this book better. More importantly, you helped me find my voice. And I'm eternally grateful.